T E R R Y   F A R R E L L

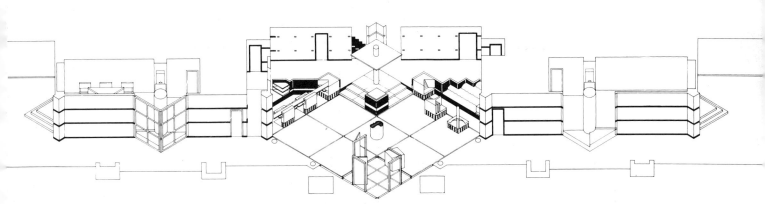

ARCHITECTURAL
Monographs

TERRY FARRELL

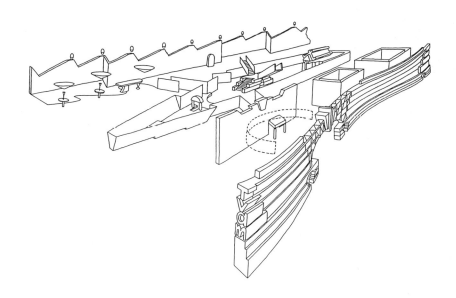

ACADEMY EDITIONS · LONDON/ST. MARTIN'S PRESS · NEW YORK

ARCHITECTURAL Monographs

Subscriptions and Editorial Offices:
7/8 Holland Street, London W8
Tel: 01-937 6996

Publisher:
Dr. Andreas Papadakis

Editor:
Frank Russell

Page 1: Television Studios 1982-83, axonometric of entrance

Page 2: Television Broadcasting Centre 1981-82, interior

Page 3: Television Broadcasting Centre 1981-82, perspective of major design elements

Page 6: Television Studios 1982-83, entrance front

Published in Great Britain in 1984 by
Academy Editions 7/8 Holland Street London W8
Copyright © 1984 Architectural Monographs
and Academy Editions

Published in the United States of America in 1984 by
St. Martin's Press 175 Fifth Avenue New York NY 10010

Library of Congress Catalog Card Number 84-50884
ISBN 0 312 79286 7 (USA only)

Typeset by Capital Setters Ltd., London W1
Printed and bound in Hong Kong

Contents

FOREWORD

It is a fitting tribute to the memory of a great architect that the idea for this Architectural Monograph first arose as a topic of conversation at the Dulwich Picture Gallery on the occasion of the launch of the Soane Monograph in the Spring of 1983. At the time Farrell was, of course, too busy with the *genius loci* to be much interested in discussion; but in the time that has elapsed since then we have collaborated with the Partnership to produce this first complete and up to date presentation of the buildings and projects — and thinking — of this leading English architect, one who has been hailed as Britain's premier Post-Modernist.

During a professional career which has now spanned over two crucial decades, Farrell has shown a distinct line of development from the fundamentalism he was taught as a student by Louis Kahn to his present-day radical eclecticism, an experience summarised by Farrell in his autobiographical essay 'Hedgehogs and Foxes'. It is this very quality of change — of adaptability and responsiveness — which makes Farrell's career of interest to contemporaries, (one which Colin Amery sees as a microcosm of modernism itself) and this contributes in no small measure to his success, if success can be reckoned in terms of the number of major commissions now under way and popularity with the public.

In the first of four essays, Farrell himself assesses the state of British architecture 'after modernism', surveying the panoply of architecture in Britain since the early 60s. Discussing, in turn, problems of change, patronage, tradition and collective memory, 'gentle' and 'anecdotal' architecture, romantic and expressive technology, and, ultimately, the state — and future — of British architecture after modernism, he sees his own experience developing from a belief in a centralising philosophy to the freer and joyous practise of architecture. In personal terms this has led from an experimentation with mass production and systems building, to rehabilitation and conservation projects, and, most recently, to the adoption of an inclusivist design approach integrating contextualism, ad hocism and collage. To conclude this two-part essay the architect presents a pictorial analysis of the human figure as primary generator of architectural form, with conceptual sketches taken from his own notebooks illustrating some of the precepts that inform his work.

In his writings Farrell demonstrates the broad scope of his interests and anxieties, and especially a genuine concern with the quality of life and the means to achieve it. As with the written word, so is Farrell in practice: one who has the enviable qualities of charismatic leadership, able to involve and inspire those around him; of seeing a positive challenge where others can see only problems; of one who has the courage of his convictions — and the *right* convictions to begin with — and to speak out where others remain silent, to name but a few. These qualities are also germaine to his work, and a wealth of solutions and approaches to the problem-solving process of architectural composition are illustrated in the buildings and projects which follow.

Housing, offices, pavilions, industrial buildings, and studios are some of the building types featured, and involving sometimes sensitive conservation and rehabilitation as well as new build. These illustrated works concentrate on the very short period of Farrell's independence as the Terry Farrell Partnership though there is also a summary of work undertaken in partnership with Nicholas Grimshaw 1965-80.

Credits for job responsibilities are included in the project description in each case, but for a fuller explanation of the workings of the office see page 116. Each project is illustrated with presentation drawings and occasional conceptual sketches, together with photographs in both colour and black and white which have been painstakingly compiled over the years, many of which are published for the first time: it is typical of the Partnership that progress on site has been so thoroughly and well documented, and that leading British architectural photographers have been commissioned.

In 'Pragmatic Art and Spatial Virtuosity' Colin Amery traces Farrell's career from his school days through the encounters with Brave New World technology and partnership with Grimshaw to the 'gentle pragmatism' found in current projects. In looking at the context of the work, Amery identifies the complex nature of the architect's dilemma, and sees in Farrell, with contemporaries like Dixon and Gough, the birth of a movement with a new architectural language.

Charles Jencks, in 'Farrell Moves Towards Symbolism', explores the sources of Farrell's Post-Modern Classicism which has superceded his earlier 'expedient tech' style. A postscript records their collaboration on the private house, and the resulting influence on their ideas.

Both writers share the opinion that not only is Farrell a talented architect and urban theorist to whom critical acclaim has come early, but also that the best work is yet to come; in Colin Amery's words, Farrell is an architect 'with a major future'.

Frank Russell

7

BRITISH ARCHITECTURE AFTER 'MODERNISM'
Terry Farrell

'A new regionalism . . . exists as part of the unconscious ideologies which underlie current practice and is connected with the actual political-economic situation whose modalities are only indirectly related to any supposedly indigenous culture. It is the result of a complex interaction between modern international capitalism and various national traditions which are enshrined in institutions and ingrained attitudes. . . It is precisely because the ingredients of contemporary architecture are so similar all over the "developed" world that the slight differences of interpretation to which they are subjected in different countries are so interesting.'[1]

Alan Colquhoun

Ironically, mainstream British architects are uniquely reluctant to examine any threads of regionalism in their current work. International modernism is still enthusiastically promoted by official bodies such as the R.I.B.A. as much to convince them that Britain is keeping pace internationally on the economic and political front as for any utopian socialist reasons; the Welfare State idealism of post-war Britain persuaded many architects to pursue the original ideological link of socialism and modernism — but in 1984 it's the government of Thatcherite conservatism that is most likely to equate modernism with productive efficiency and economic progress.

Loyalty to this interpretation of modernism is a peculiar aspect of current British 'regionalism' which frequently gets in the way of seeing what is really most relevant here. In his 'regionalism' article, Colquhoun makes some perceptive observations about British High-Tech architecture about which he concludes that: 'An architecture which aims at a transcendental and utopian vision of technology can, perhaps, be seen in Freudian terms, as a displacement'. The British have a national attitude of disliking change — as is obvious in their maintaining the shell of so many customs and institutions long after their relevance has vanished. Within such a climate, change that does take place is often ignored as though it isn't happening, or else it happens along the lines of the High-Tech 'displace-ment' diagnosis of Colquhoun.

Recently a small number of architect selection procedures for nationally important projects have caused quite a stir, probably because they have given a public stage to the issue of how well we are coming to terms with changed values, though in each — Vauxhall Cross, the National Gallery and the B.B.C. Radio Headquarters — the forces of conservative modernism eventually prevailed for oddly insular reasons. It often seems in this country that the only way to confront the demands of progress is to change radically the appearance of everything, a procedure which satisfies the need to keep things as they are

whilst placating those that emphasise the need for progress.

For the British appearances are held, invariably hypocritically, to be everything — an attitude which goes with a long-established and entrenched culture which firstly does not value the genuinely visual and is more verbal in its communication skills and cultural preferences, and secondly reflects a national mis-alignment of, or confusion over, the interface of appearance and reality, language and content. The core of the 'regional' problem of British architecture is how to identify 'real' change and then how to reconcile 'real' change with the undoubtedly attractive and valuable existing environment.

The genuine fear of the conservationists is that modern architecture has been so often concerned with just the appearance of change; to take just one example, whole areas of beautiful Georgian and Victorian 'slum' buildings in cities like Liverpool, London and Glasgow have been demolished to be replaced by blocks of flats unmistakably 'of the 20th century' with little or no change or improvement in the lot of the residents who have merely been swopped from a familiar (invariably aesthetically considered) brick slum to an unfamiliar (invariably aesthetically ignorant) concrete slum. The modernists, on the other hand, fear the innate British resistance to change will lead to no progress being made in developing and adjusting itself in a changing world. Both the left and the right here have opportunistically aligned them-selves with modernism since both agree that environmental change achieves political goals, albeit in quite opposing ways: socialism with social restructuring through schemes such as massive public housing, and conservatism with profit-motivated private enterprise schemes such as offices and shopping, to achieve a more economically competitive society. Each party sees the others' environmental aims as anathema, and so just as our post-war pendulum politics consistently neutralise real change there has not emerged any clear national policy at a political level — though there has been an emergence of converging grass-roots attitudes to environmental issues which has arisen independently of political parties and their close allies, the architectural establishment (for the latter a higher rate of any kind of change often means more business). To be fair, appearances to an extent do affect attitude to change; a classic example is that although the power of the British Monarchy may have given way politically to Parliament, the appearance of its preservation does affect the British attitude to politics (because governments come and go, politicians are rather unimportant, lesser people compared with the 'permanent' Monarchy), a fantasy which could be seen as self-fulfilling. An architecture of the H.G.

Wells' futurist type is so obviously an over-reaction rather than a solution to the problems of Britain's historic environment, though this syndrome is not unique to Britain; (underdeveloped countries want airports, High-Tech hospitals and Holiday Inns before housing and industry) and is very much linked to the twin fantasies of crisis cultivation and the equation of technology with progress.

Architectural Patronage in the U.K.

'The demand that all buildings should become works of architecture... is strictly offensive to common sense... one might possibly stipulate that architecture is a social institution related to building in much the same way that literature is to speech.'[2]

Colin Rowe

In Britain more than twice as many buildings are designed by architects than in the wealthier construction climate of the United States (and incidentally it is frequently said that there are more architects in Hampstead than there are in India). Somehow the Welfare State has proliferated senior professionals — doctors, university teachers, architects, barristers — ahead of actual everyday need, with the effect of debasing professionalism and bureaucratising relationships with clients. Architects' training has now become in large part a preparation for bureaucracy: over 50% of U.K. architects are government employed, and many private commissions originate from the clients' need for help in getting through endless regulations and official approvals.

The State has also been a very good provider to private architects — in the fifties and sixties in particular the building boom was fuelled by new universities, hospitals, new towns, housing estates, town halls and libraries. In the meantime so very few private sector commissions were carried out by recognised architects — large numbers of shopping centres and offices were carried out almost entirely by commercial architects with mean architectural aspirations. Although some of the surviving and respected architects from those days still get prestige government-financed work (Lasdun at the National Theatre, Casson at the Houses of Parliament extension, Powell & Moya at the International Conference Centre) the seventies' generation has had to develop relationships with industry and commerce to get work, due to the severe run-down of state-financed projects over the last ten years.

One of the problems with the private sector here is that a very considerable proportion of buildings are built 'speculatively' by developers rather than by owner/occupiers (especially when compared with, say, Germany, Japan or the U.S.). The British origins of this tradition probably lie in the great land holdings, both rural and urban, of the aristocratic estates — and even today the key figures are called 'estate agents' (which in U.S. parlance means real estate brokers). The present-day financiers and investors of the City of London have an attitude to buildings in which they perceive them of necessity as anonymous commodities to be managed on a large scale like farming. From this emerges a 'rotation of crops' investment cycle from private house building to hotels to offices to industry which leads the construction industry to have to follow a zigzag path (often related to changes in government), from shortage to excess to shortage in each of these building types. Investment money is in this way concerned with the anonymity of property and not with users, processes or identifiable companies — in the ultra-conservative and pessimistic belief that property and land are more secure than people, production processes and individual enterprise. Property investment of this kind tends to have none of the pride of ownership and concern for environment and quality that many of the great urban family estates exemplified (like those of Bedford, Portland and Westminster). More often now, investment is from pension fund or insurance and banking sources which hold portfolios; knowledge of environmental qualities and context is virtually irrelevant except insofar as there is a short-term return on investment, a process which in the long-term must result in the gradual run-down of property and land values along with quality of environment (ironically confirming that property and landowners have ultimately more to gain financially from town planning controls, against which they invariably lead the complaints, than any other sector of the community).

Where there has been a change in the private sector is the emergence of several more concerned and identity-proud (though smaller-scale) developers in the eighties and in the influence of American industry buildings here. Some observers have dubbed 1983 the 'year of the tenant' — i.e. the year that the post-war sellers' market ended. A new generation of developers is responding with factories and offices that are 'user'-orientated. In the U.S. there is a long tradition of companies identifying themselves through their buildings. Not only do commercial companies like Johnson's Wax, Cummins, and General Motors invest in good building but cities become identifiable through company-built edifices that carry their name — Manhattan, for example, with its Chrysler, Woolworth and Rockefeller Center buildings, and now the AT&T. There is no such tradition in the U.K. though recent new buildings by American companies here have set new standards in industrial buildings — Cummins (again), Herman Miller, I.B.M. and Digital, for example. However, these are constructed in very limited numbers and away from the urban areas where the major environmental issues prevail. Real urban improvement has been left to very small groups, usually of historic conservationist or left-wing persuasion who have operated primarily to nullify the worst excesses rather than to promote new work. Socialism has contributed to the urban environment in

Europe more successfully than here, partly due to our more tenuous urban traditions which have led to enthusiasm for improvement being diverted back to the countryside in the form of New Towns and the like – all very much to the detriment of quality in the old urban centres.

With such an insufficient tradition of patronage, good British architects today often have great difficulty in finding a path which ensures a consistent flow of good building projects. On the academic front the schools of architecture are distinctly and depressingly separated from practice, and in spite of claims to the contrary this is a trend which is increasing during the current laying-off of higher education staff where those that are part-time or have outside interests are the first to go. In many other countries (e.g. the U.S. and Germany) the link between practice and teaching at key institutions has obvious benefits inasmuch as one stimulates the other, and it is frequently the source of new commissions (as many eminent U.S. architects, and indeed recently our own James Stirling, have discovered to their benefit). Virtually the only supporter on a broad front of the employment of good architects is the R.I.B.A. – which does an energetic job in disseminating commissions from the very smallest to the largest – but this institutionalisation of commissions is not without its disadvantages for the client, as well as for the architect (particularly those who do not agree with the prevailing institutionalised concepts of what is good and bad architecture).

Public Image of Architects versus Public Image of Architecture

For some time now the informed British public has been ahead of official architecture in genuine concern for the environment, a concern usually expressed in the form of conservationism. The demolition of the Euston Arch was the symbol for many of the last act of public vandalism that was to be accepted without much of a fight. There have since been significant successes for conservationism against large-scale planning and modernism – notably at Covent Garden, Spitalfields, Bristol, Liverpool and London Docklands, along with many housing associations and small developers who have rehabilitated large areas of historic buildings rather than redevelop them. Most conservationists among the public are not primarily preservationists but rather have a genuine concern for the quality of life afforded by our environment, a fact architects opposed to conservation frequently refuse to recognise.

Inevitably the national press depicts architects as vandals, and public grievance is not abated by the intransigence of the architects' official line on modernism: that great architecture was always unpopular, an argument bereft of factual accuracy as well as insight into one of the original and essential

arguments for international modernism – that it was to be non-elitist and the 20th century architecture of the people! Popular feeling is very strongly against what architects do, a reality which in a democratic society like ours cannot be brushed aside. Architecture cannot exist independently of the main flow of social history. What now of Mies' dictum that architecture should be 'the will of the epoch'? One national journalist wrote recently that he would one day just rush out and kill an architect – 'any architect' and then adds that he believes he would certainly be acquitted of murder as it would be seen as a crime *'for humanity'*.[3] Another in *The Times* wrote that the only people who are not distressed by what modern architects do are those 'that are led by a dog and that carry a white stick'.[4] There is an emerging concern among many architectural historians of environmental qualities of a broader kind than those immediately identifiable as historic, what Andrew Saint calls 'the aesthetic art historical standard, so simple and easy to apply, is having to gradually give way to murkier and even more complex methods of evaluation, to concepts of "group value", adaptability and community use. This is more nearly the language of ecology than that of traditional architectural history.'[5] Marcus Binney of 'Save Britain's Heritage' and *Country Life* has initiated three major reappraisals of the London sites at Billingsgate, Battersea and recently Mansion House. Similarly the socialist G.L.C. has sponsored 'the people's' alternative schemes throughout London (e.g. Coin Street and Hammersmith Broadway).

The current Thatcher government support for modernism is no doubt motivated by the concept of architecture as being part of a society which is the product of economic determinism. But how can any architect not be sympathetic to many earlier communities – when in periods of military and economic stability architecture as an expressive art form was seen as a prime end product and buildings were secondarily means of enclosure, defence, production and even comfort? The aim was to be 'non-productive', in our terms, and labour intensiveness was a positive goal – a way of life committed to building buildings – a very appealing notion when compared with the contradiction of our labour-saving construction methods and mass unemployment. Unemployment as a result of economic equations must be the leading nonsense of our time and an architecture which takes factory production methods as its inspiration is particularly obscene in this context as it ignores so much about what makes up the quality of life. Historically an excess of human resources over essential life-supporting tasks was seen as a time of opportunity when excess was channelled into creative production as an end in itself. We probably have enough new buildings in quantitative terms – enclosure is not an urgent issue even though politically from time to time it is manipulated to seem so. The environmental problems and opportunities we have

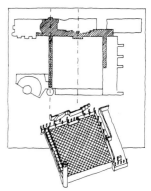

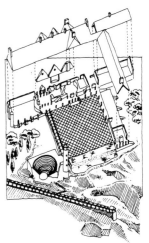

1 Ralph Lerner and Richard Reid, Villa Vasone Studies, 1981

2 Sir Clough Williams-Ellis, Portmeirion, 1926-66, Battery Square

3 A.W.N. Pugin and Sir Charles Bary, Houses of Parliament, 1840-60

are qualitative ones — architecture should now be more intensive and indeed extravagant in human (though not other!) resources, particularly in terms of craftsmanship, thought and care — and upon the drawing board as much as anywhere! There is evidence that architecture in its broadest sense is, in Britain, very probably *the* most 'popular' art form. If this is so, then the enthusiasm and energy that goes into, say, home improvements and tourist trips to great historic buildings ought (in a time of excess, material wealth and unemployment) to be more effectively tapped by the profession to support a more vital and creative architecture.

Anecdotal Architecture

The literary traditions of this country as much as anything stem from the natural reliance on words rather than visual signs to communicate. A comparison of the much more limited French with the extensive and rich English vocabulary demonstrates the extent to which French communication relies on the self-expressive gestural vocabulary of the communicator — the more reserved British fall back on a 'words only' approach and the verbal, literary and anecdotal traditions in all aspects of our culture (including architecture) are extraordinarily deep-rooted. Grouped buildings which break down the mass of

single statements in a multiplicity of linked passages of information are good examples of this tradition. The Houses of Parliament themselves form a village of buildings from different periods with several fronts, and several bits are known by quite independent and separate names like characters in a novel; typically undue emphasis is given to quite gratuitous elements, such as the clock tower Big Ben and the air duct housing in the Victoria Tower. Oxford and Cambridge colleges, the Garden City movement, the Smithsons' housing and economist buildings, Clough Williams Ellis and Portmeirion are all building groups that have their own script and plot and their own accompanying narrators. Currently Lerner and Reid (as coincidentally their names might suggest!) explore this tradition in their vernacular and Vasone villa studies as does Will Alsop in his work at Riverside and elsewhere (his work appeared in a recent *AD* article under the appropriate title of a 'pictorial diary').[6] The use of collage, multiplicity of images, dispersal of forms to create village or mini-city massing, episodic diversions into detail en route, the love of repetition of an understood vocabulary, the instinct not to arrive but to enjoy much more the journey (Chaucer-style) are all anecdotal or narrative in structure and attitude. The labyrinthine narrative is a particularly exciting format: great buildings like Street's City of London Law Courts and Waterhouse's Manchester Town Hall, as well as

4 Alsop, Barnett and Lyall, Riverside Studios, 1981

5 Campbell, Zogolovitch, Wilkinson and Gough, Lutyens Exhibition, Hayward Gallery, 1981
6 Jeremy Dixon, Maida Vale housing, 1983

whole areas of cities such as London, Chester and Edinburgh elaborately avoid the formal urban patterns of Europe or America. Colin Rowe reflected this particular British tendency when he refers to buildings generally as 'speech' and architecture specifically as 'literature'.[7]

Perhaps in the freedom from strict conventions of expression, i.e. the styles of classical, Gothic, modern etc, the scope of expression is radically opened up. There is a case for arguing that some of the most fluent buildings are those between or outside of 'movements', a case which may be made for what is now happening at the end of the 20th century. Linguistic studies have demonstrated that not only does the mode of communication limit the content but also our very cognitive and emotional range. One of the problems of this time after modernism is that modernism itself handed down a grammar of indeterminancy and gave us a system for assembling sentences without a predetermined hierarchy or vocabulary of usable words.

Tradition and Collective Memory

The city as depository of history and collective memory is closely linked to anecdotal architecture insofar as historical threads can make intrinsic and vivid elements of any such narrative; it is nevertheless a separate character thread of the history-loving British who immortalise tradition rather readily in appearances. Scratch the surface of any plot of land in England and there is a story to tell, one which intensifies in urban centres and particularly in London. Beneath the Mansion House site of the proposed Mies van der Rohe tower block is the old stream, the Walbrook; Romans built the Temple of Mithras there, medieval street patterns and street names still survive and the side wall of Wren's Church of St Stephen's Walbrook dropped straight down into the stream. None of this is irrevocably lost. In small and large ways history emerges up to the surface of the present physical expression of land and buildings. To make new buildings and urban spaces which reinforce this history can only benefit both new and old, a layering process of accumulated benefit like pearl growth. A

commitment to conserving historical memories and patterns adds immeasurably to our lives and the arguments for their demolition on the grounds of 'progress' are quite indefensible; if technology can do so much, it should be able to conserve with ease what there is left of the past. If technology is to add to our lives, then a route via destruction cannot be justified because it impoverishes us. In Britain and even London there are easily enough new building sites with opportunities that don't involve compromising historical continuity; additionally most modern processes can, with imagination and ingenuity, be very efficiently housed in historic environments without destroying them. In parallel it is now increasingly demonstrated by concerned architects and planners that low technology, ecologically concerned urban schemes that consider microclimate, passive energy strategies, less separation and specialisation of building type and mix are where the future of our efficient urban centres lies (e.g. Richard MacCormac's Spitalfields' study).

Engulfed by so much residual evidence of history, a real problem does exist for the British of reconciliation of past with future but the challenge of this conflict gives direction and real architectural opportunity. There are differing views of the past and different weightings given to what remains, but the only genuinely uncreative interpretation is that which argues that the collective memory needs to be erased in order to progress — to recommend denial is, as even Hollywood cowboys remind us, 'running away from oneself'.

Modern architecture has added to our language and had a useful if puritanical purging effect, but its rejection of the status quo and therefore history alienated the movement from cities and urbanism. It is in this area where it has most clearly failed. That is why urbanism and the related considerations of conservationism, contextualism and regionalism are the most potent 'after modernism' forces acting for a new alignment of architecture — more so than any new politics of architecture (Rationalism etc) or any purely stylistic or decorative architecture (Post-Modern Classicism).

7 John Outram, Kensal Road
factories, 1978-80
8 Ted Cullinan, Mark Beedle and
Alan Short, St Mary's Church,
Barnes, 1978-80

Gentle Architecture

'and gentleness, in hearts at peace, under an English heaven'[8]

Rupert Brooks

The British, isolated from continental wars and revolutionary upheavals, have relatively unfortified urban settlements which spread out into a countryside which is soft and relaxed with no extremes. By comparison with so many other countries, even our violence is restrained and quiet – compare Agatha Christie's and our TV detective stories with anything coming from America with its murder-a-minute routine. Piers Gough's comment that he would like to build a 'pretty' architecture that 'my grandmother would like' is a knowing, self-deprecating acknowledgment of how British architects relish an unaggressive, unassertive and loved architecture, which has its modern roots in Britain's very own architectural movement, namely Arts and Crafts. (Gough's lovingly prepared and very popular Lutyens exhibition was one of the most delightful exhibition designs London has seen and was all the more successful because it civilised the brutish and banal interiors of the Hayward Gallery. It was suggested by many people – to no avail – that the exhibition interior should remain as the permanent backdrop to all future exhibitions.)

Even the most assertive periods of imported modernism are milder versions of the original things from overseas; Roehampton pales beside the fascist megalomania of Ville Radieuse, the Hertfordshire schools are examples of relatively humane system buildings, Britain's Miesian city at Milton Keynes is slowly being mellowed with encircling rings of sweet brick and tile, new vernacular housing.

'Gentle architecture' implies that it is accessible and understandable to a wide range of people; is non-alienating in contextual handling and external expression of internal use and in entrance ways; is unassertive and familiar in colour, form, imagery and formality of arrangement, sane and humane in terms of non-extreme theoretical or technological interpretations; and is above all an anxiety-free architecture

which doesn't feed off any crisis cultivation. Endless doom predictions have fuelled politicians as well as architects to make insensitive, hasty decisions about architecture and the environment. A persuasive side effect of technological adaptation equates human decision-making with the speed and efficiency of machine processing; one lesson of the last 30 years is that if we are building appropriately for the future then *time* to think and get it right is paramount: this needs calm and moderation in action and then the ability to make decisions which can be amended en route and accept adaptations after execution.

The most obvious examples of the characteristic of gentleness in British buildings today are generally in housing and instances are Dixon's North Kensington and Maida Vale schemes with their mildly mannered reinterpretation of urban London terraced housing and James Gowan's private houses are determinedly unassertive. John Outram's decorated factory forms, and Ted Cullinan's friendly adaptations and add-ons of existing buildings all demonstrate a delightful lightness of touch.

The conservation movement, vernacular revivalism and in fact any return to applied decoration is broadly seen here as 'non-modern' in a rigidly exclusive interpretation not applied, say, in Scandinavia. The motivation for these variations varies from populism to commercial interests which want quick planning consents. Often such work is pretty sloppy and badly designed and at its very worst shows the Achilles heel of British gentleness – the search for good manners and gentility readily supersedes originality and freshness. As Adrian Stokes wrote in 'A Game Which Must Be Lost': 'the true artist is never genteel, though the servant and interpreter of urban culture. He borrows something from the countryman's out-of-door attitudes, applies them to the admitted conflicts of polite society. But art itself is not supremely a polite activity nor is a strong enthusiasm for it altogether "good form".'[9] The problem for the inexpressive British is that the balance is almost too delicately poised between the institutionalisation of manners as a regulating group influence and gentleness as a positive expression of controlled creative aggression.

Collective Expression and Individual Expression

If the dispersal of our institutions in built form, e.g. Parliament, B.B.C., Oxbridge colleges, all speak of grouped working rather than great solo performances, so British architecture seems to work best in informal design and planning groups sans manifestos or indeed strong leadership. At its best the group approach is represented by the Arts and Crafts and Garden City movements, Tecton, the old L.C.C. and some of our New Towns' design teams. Natural reliance on debating all issues and forming committees has achieved good environmental standards as a norm —but ironically individual artistic expression is not seen as normal and often therefore (in the nicest possible way of course) it is considered anti-social. The institutionalising effect of boarding schools, the Welfare State and our free state higher education system reinforces the view that the system is tolerant, fair, flexible and workable and therefore it is discourteous and disrespectful to step outside it.

It goes without saying that to do so is the essential duty of the artist; invariably, of course, if he or she is successful then he or she becomes institutionalised.

Although it is two centuries since Soane began his career and one-and-a-half since he died, his work probably receives a wider international respect now than at any time during his lifetime or since his death. Why is this and what does our time have in common with his? His rise from bricklayer's son to architect to the Bank of England is more akin to today's social mobility than that of his own time, and one encouraging note for today is that he built his best buildings during a recession in the construction industry after the Napoleonic Wars. His greatest strength, Summerson concluded, came from his architectural self-reliance. He developed a personal approach to proportion, decoration and overall style which is recognisably his alone even though he worked well within the general architectural languages of his time. Lutyens' character was probably developed into its independent foxy mould by having, through poor health, to stay at home with his mother and sisters during his childhood whilst all his brothers went away to boarding school. Mackintosh was, at his peak, never part of the British art scene and James Stirling has created quite a role from seeming bloody-mindedly independent (to the extent that at the Tate Gallery foundation ceremony his casual footwear when meeting royalty attracted as much attention as the fact that he was getting his first British commission for over a decade). These are mild deviations by most social standards, and to digress more, it is no doubt thought by architects, would probably result in no more work.[10] Many architects here stand apart from practice with pride and establish mildly theoretical, utopian or conversational positions which are adjusted into retreat when there is ever a likelihood of *actually* building. In other art forms the life of a recluse or actively anti-social animal is more attainable; Dylan Thomas, George Orwell, Oscar Wilde, D.H. Lawrence and many others all showed that heroes in literature here are permitted (in retrospect, at least) much more deviant anti-social behaviour. But architects have to come to grips with society in order to build and if there is anything to be learnt from European or American architects, it is that self-reliance and individual interpretation enrich society's architecture.

If some aggression is an essential component of creativity, what natural source is there in British society which can stir its lassitude? There is so much benefit to those still privileged in our class-entrenched society in staying ahead that hidden aggression — gentlemanly behaviour whilst holding on — has been developed with consummate skill. Obviously explicit aggression is seen in our unique soccer madness, recent urban riots, and youth cultures of pop and punk. The vitality of punk culture is the unexpressed voice of people (in a very visual way) who are not included in the formal (and visually stereotyped) arts such as the operatic, balletic culture of the London middle classes (these two art forms still get the lion's share of government arts' funding and only less than 4% goes on visual arts). There are no British architectural equivalents of punk simply because architecture here is still so rigidly middle-class, but punk and pop represent acknowledgements of cultural influences welling up from everyday experience of people outside the normal institutionalising influence. The result is a surprisingly rich, eclectic and, above all, visual mixture. The class and cultural mix of Britain does have untapped channels of considerable range, not the great melting pot of the U.S.A. but still a strange kind of stew which surprises even those familiar with its interpretive potential. If pop and punk represent respectively the sixties' and seventies' restless creative upsurges, they were preceded by the generation of Osborne's angry young men, with the kitchen sink dramas in theatre and film, Bratby paintings, and 'Bowellism' in architecture as well as the 'Brutalism' of the Smithsons, Stirling and Gowan.

It does seem that most of these surges of activity focus on London where Britain's energetic young migrate to, and it is where Dutch and Middle Eastern constructivists (Rem Koolhaas and Zaha Hadid) meet immigrant American critic observers (Charles Jencks et al), Czech refugee High-Techers (Jiricna and Kaplicky), Greek and French theorists and so on. But these are foreigners who come to London as a meeting place of foreignness, who meet against the backdrop of our mellow, kindly, likeable architectural scene and bring with them the necessary friction in-built from their culture of origin. The native-born have to develop their own 'in-built-friction-to-stimulate'. The easiest and most traditional route to achieve this is to overcome the insular comforts by becoming a quasi-foreigner, and from the Grand Tour onwards

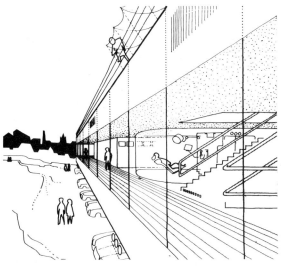

9 Cedric Price, Potteries Think Belt, 1966, edge of battery housing block

bringing 'it' back from overseas has been a certain way to get the creative juices and commissions flowing, as Inigo Jones, Robert Adam, John Soane and very many painters and poets did. Recent imports, though, rather than being a stimulus, have something of a passive inferiority complex about their adoption. A repeated argument in favour of the proposed Mies tower in the City is that at a stroke it would become the greatest 20th-century building in Britain — which apart from ignoring so much native architecture ignores all the realities of context, appropriateness etc as a basis for assessing a piece of architecture. Le Corbusier today is no longer so revered here (cf. the U.S.A.) simply because of what his protagonists so blindly built; like certain French wines, Le Corbusier never travelled well, and exposed concrete and wide open spaces between buildings with empty ground floors are particularly unsuited to our wet and windy climate. Today the technologically-infatuated, of course, import from America and there is an ever accelerating belief that where the U.S. is today we will be there tomorrow — a kind of 'if you want to get ahead, think Yankee' syndrome. This belief when viewed in worldwide terms doesn't look quite so rock-solid, and there is a view which is becoming increasingly attractive that the future has been better anticipated by smaller, more introverted countries that achieve mature social and cultural integration with low growth. James Robertson in his book *The Sane Alternative* characterises these two options as the HE (Hyper-Expansionist) and the SHE (Sane, Humane, Ecological).[11] The future of Britain must be all about achieving the latter; the inevitable failure of technological determinism was well stated by Cedric Price in his lecture title 'Technology is the answer but what was the question?'

Romantic and Decorative Technology

The marriage of engineering and art at the Bauhaus bred an architecture that was inspired by the factory and the machine. It was butch and assertive, and valued the rational above any sentiment or as Mies put it: 'we do not respect flights of the spirit as much as we value reason and realism'.[12] The civilising of this

potentially insensitive and aggressive movement has been continuous and apostates are invariably recognised by true believers by the fact that they actually preferred their buildings to be liked (i.e. rather than for their buildings to do people good). But in spite of swings and changes in modernism's own concept of itself, the only true modernism remains the undiluted essence of the twenties, within each swing and change since have been all the ingredients of Post-Modernism. The Scandinavians were the first to develop a kinder and more regional variation. The Welfare State architects in Britain in the fifties were determinedly anti-monumental and the search was on for systems with a human face (Clasp), modernism that could adapt to historical settings (Powell & Moya at Oxbridge) as well as work inspired by the later apostate work of Le Corbusier (Stirling and Gowan, Howell, Killick etc).

But the sixties saw quite a radical swing to yet another interpretation which allowed for personal expression and a human face to modernism — early High-Tech which took its inspiration from Bucky Fuller with his whacky mid-West self-reliance rather than the ideology of the Bauhaus, and had Price and Ehrenkrantz as its heroes. Super technology as a backdrop was the theme with repeated images of intensively hyperactive foregrounds of trendy pop people inside super-serviced all-purpose space. The engineering was a fantasy — the improvement it made to one's lifestyle was everything — and certainly the engineering itself was only vaguely there. As an architecture it was non-monumental and non-intrusive, indeed almost anti-building. Mathematical grids, system building, relationships between servicing and space were to be exploited as a dynamic for user and not architectural expression. If there is continuity of this thinking in anti-modernist feeling today, it is that the technology did become feasible, and therefore no longer the issue: the problem became how to develop the very life and character in architectural expression which the sixties saw as the easy bit. In other words, the seeds of recognition that modernism's technological anonymity was not the basis for creating a balanced and complete environment were already there in the sixties. It is interesting that the architectural school at the A.A. which was the centre of much of this early 'High-Tech-backdrop' approach did not naturally progress, as some of its pupils and followers did, into the modernist High-Tech monumentalism of the seventies and early eighties but developed a range of styles and ideas which in the main accepted that modernism had ended.

The late seventies and early eighties modernists' assimilation of the essentially British development of High-Tech responded to the need to focus more on the building as an object and clients as commercially motivated: the days of the Welfare State big budget government projects had ended. A kind of business-man's technological expressionism that used many of

10 Archigram (Peter Cook),
Bournemouth Nets Project, 1966
11 Eva Jiricna, Belsize Park·Flat,
1983

the original Bauhaus arguments and returned to a more aggressive and butch no-nonsense approach emerged: that it was not publicly liked was seen as a puritanical confirmation of its modern movement lineage. Buildings that communicate 'bits of bridges stuck together' or 'all pipes, guts and structures on the outside' (two lay comments at the 1983 Royal Academy Architecture Exhibition) express an engineering rather than an architectural language and are menacing and intrusive rather than a backdrop.

When Bucky first caught the eye of the establishment here in the sixties it was often said that his work displayed a kind of lateral thinking engineering, but 'was it real architecture?' Today it seems the U.K. establishment's acceptance of this engineering-inspired architecture leads one to ask 'all right, but is it relevant engineering?' Much of it is, in the end, pastiche engineering. There is a more relevant continuity with Bucky's broad, responsible thinking being maintained today by suggesting that 'more with less' often means the least technology to do the job well. A lot of technology may be needed for some tasks but it's the way the problem is posed that separates the technologically dazzled from the real problem-solvers. Architecture's isolated and pristine homages to technological advance contrast with the same advance fundamentally eroding the quality of life for us all in the air we breathe, our drinking water, our food and even human birth itself.

Bucky, of course, worked with Louis Kahn who in turn had as one of his closest design partners (the engineer, Le Ricolais) to make an architecture that was neither a backdrop nor a mere 'tool' but an active ingredient of life itself which integrated the disciplines in an intuitive rather than mechanistic or systematic way. 'A dome is not conceived when questions arise how to build it. Nervi grows an arch, Fuller grows a dome', said Louis Kahn.[13]

Relevant architectural engineering can fundamentally restructure how buildings work without preconceptions over appearance — as does, say, passive solar architecture — and can integrate architecture and engineering in great art as Kahn did; the resultant language is not aggressively butch or uncomfortably

intrusive but related to people's feelings as well as their needs and is altogether gentler, kinder and much more lovable.

Due to economic decline and the means to capitalise on inventions through economic growth, the British today are more infatuated with technology than seriously interested in it. Archigram, wire bird cages by Lord Snowdon, the Comet and Concorde and of course the best aspects of the High-Tech school have an essentially *romantic approach to technology*. (Colin Rowe described Archigram as 'townscape in a **spacesuit**'.[14]) If the roots of this romanticism were more clearly acknowledged, romantic and expressive High-Tech and other engineering-inspired art forms would become less self-serious and utopian, and would help develop an architecture which was more relaxed, joyous and celebratory, and could as much as any other route bring people to relate to modernism in architecture again. There is in the U.K. an established group of architects who have relationships with manufacturers, industrial designers and our excellent engineers that refine and make much more elegant the underlying engineering programmes of our buildings; Peter Rice's structures with Rogers at Quimper and Princetown come to mind, as well as Eva Jiricna's interiors and Michael Hopkins' house and tent structures. The more zany and futuristic and/or temporary the architecture, the more sensuous it seems to be, like Jan Kaplicky and David Nixon's drawings and Mark Fisher's temporary structures for Pink Floyd's itinerant pop concerts.

A more expressive technology is very much part of an architecture which follows on after modernism; the obsessive overlaying of historical cultural references of American Post-Modern Classicism is an expression of cultural anxiety out of place here in Britain, though I should add such overstatements certainly have made the British shake out of their lethargy a bit. The European tradition, particularly of Arts and Crafts and Art Nouveau, took so much of its inspiration from how things were made; the studded wall cladding of Otto Wagner, the elaborate but prefabricated cast-iron elements of Hector Guimard's metro stations and the sculptured RSJs of C.R. Mackintosh were all outstanding combinations of art and technology. In the thirties our best 'modern' British architecture did not depend too blindly on the International Style and demonstrated a less doctrinaire, more personal and decorative mix of architecture and technology, such as Owen Williams' black glass and chrome *Daily Express* building, Emberton's playful use of reinforced concrete at Blackpool Casino and Holden's underground stations. The scope for a more humane and decorative technology is even greater today with the potentialities of new glazed walls that have such a wide performance range and come in so many colours and reflectances, frames and non-frames; translucent fabric structures that make acres of roofing powerful sources of daylight; colour application processes that permanently colour steel, plastic and in fact just about anything with any colour we now like to use, and of course the application of high technology to traditional materials. An over-emphasis on utility denies so much of this palette and an over-emphasis on architecture as pure art deadens so much of the freedom with which it can be exploited.

The real lesson for British architects from American Post-Modern Classicism is that the British are too precious and overstuffy in their concerns. If British modernism's failure was that it took itself too earnestly, too joylessly and seriously, it seems inevitable that establishment modern architects prefer Quinlan Terry's 'properly done' classicism to anything freewheeling and interpretive like Venturi, Stern or Graves. The puritanical zeal underlying the reaction of establishment Britain to the frothy sensuality of Post-Modern Classicism was expressed well by Quinlan Terry who called it 'The Work of Satan'.[15]

After Modernism

An art form like architecture cannot hold onto a pose of rebellion or rejection indefinitely; reconciliations with the central drift of society inevitably set in, as action creates counter reaction. The interesting thing today about 'after', 'counter' or 'post' modernism is that they cannot be defined without first defining modernism.[16] Modernism was centralising, its ideology the 'International Style'. The counter movements are regional and the emerging dispersed foci are illuminated by contemporary architects who express their cultures like Graves, Krier, Botta, Hollein, Bofill and Isozaki. Modernism was impersonal, the architecture of anonymity; its counter reaction elevates architects with highly personal architectural visions and skill. The non-ornamental machine aesthetic is responded to with decoration and ornament; masculine drive with sensuality and sensitivity; rationalised oversimplification with complexity and contradiction; futurism with historicism; and universality of solutions with contextuality.

In the end the British may well discover that a more free-style 'after modernism' is very much their kind of architecture simply because it is so British — with its tolerant, eclectic, contextual and more romantic and open approach. Perhaps the reason for so much nervous hesitation here is that architects are faced with the dilemma that to progress means belatedly to follow much of the rest of the world which has for some time now been building upon some of the essential aspects of British architecture which we (again belatedly) rejected fifty years ago for modernism.

Notes

1 Alan Colquhoun, *Casabella*, review of the MOMA exhibition of 4 office projects, July 1983.

2 Colin Rowe and Fred Koetter, *Collage City*, MIT Press, 1978.

3 Andrew Alexander, *Daily Mail*.

4 Bernard Levin, *The Times*.

5 Andrew Saint, 'The Architect and the Architectural Historian', *RIBA Transactions 4*, 1983.

6 *British Architecture*, Architectural Design Special Issue, 1982.

7 Rowe and Koetter, *op. cit.*

8 Rupert Brooke, 'The Soldier' from *Poetical Works of Rupert Brooke*, Geoffrey Keynes, Faber and Faber, 1946.

9 Adrian Stokes, *A Game Which Must Be Lost*, Carcanet New Press, 1973.

10 My earlier comments on a 'gentle' architecture in no way should be taken as supporting 'good manners' above everything — as the British make quite a thing out of committing atrocities to children, and food as well as buildings in the name of cultivating 'good manners'.

11 James Robertson, *The Sane Alternative*, River Basin Publishers, 1980.

12 Peter Blake, *The Master Builders*, Morton, 1976.

13 Louis Kahn, *Perspecta*, The Yale magazine.

14 Rowe and Koetter, *op. cit.*

15 Quinlan Terry, 'Twentieth Century Renaissance', *Architects' Journal*, December 1983, p.40.

16 The term 'Post-Modernism' is an American invention which has become more and more associated with classical revivalism, an interpretation I personally do not accept, much preferring Ada Louise Huxtable's definition that 'Post-Modernism is simply what happens after Modernism'. 'After Modernism' (AM) has a forward-looking morning optimism that the rear-view expression 'Post-Modernism' (PM) hasn't and it is a term I prefer to use.

HEDGEHOGS AND FOXES
Terry Farrell

Isaiah Berlin once commented that people could be characterised as hedgehogs or foxes[1]. There were those with a fixed single strategy and those who survived by continuous adaptation. Since the decline in influence of doctrinaire modernism (and the rigid stances of the other-'isms' of the early part of the twentieth century) it has become more and more a time for foxes. Today to establish growth and continuity in one's personal work means responding to an ever-widening theatre of influences within an overall climate of rapid change. Progress inevitably involves the ebbing and flowing of response to these stimuli; shifting patterns emerge, come into focus, blur, fade and then return.

The curvy plastic Clifton Nurseries I greenhouse (below) returns to interests expressed in the organic High-Tech, Blackpool Climatron of 1961. The shiny, decorated, coloured add-ons on the north face of Limehouse revitalised a large old building as did the ad hoc plug-in plastic pods and service tower of the Students' Hostel of 1968. The manipulation of grids, frame and systems characterises designing with and for factory mass production whether it is for mobile homes, factories or more recently decorative curtain wall cladding. The lessons in formalism with Louis Kahn and the continuous reminders of classical traditions in architecture which keep surfacing in any restructuring of old buildings or while working in the older urban contexts have led to the re-emergence of anthropomorphism with its emphasis on bilateral symmetry and hierarchical compositions as at Vauxhall Cross and many other current projects.

In the 1950s architecture students were faced with original modernist leaders veering away from mainline modernism, as well as the emergence of new generations of post-war architects who were treading various independent routes away from modernism. But for many students the most original and independent routes were being established by those architects who were never true believers in the first place — and the inevitable home of most of these was in America, where the message of modernism in most respects came too late. The Newcastle thesis of 1961 wholeheartedly committed itself to Bucky Fuller's ideas. An existing all-in-one holiday building was to be recreated out at sea — and so the Victorian concept of the winter gardens becomes a climatron with suspended space-frame floors hung on cables from tubular steel masts, clad in gasket anti-sun glazing with moveable pneumatic rooftop structures all assembled together. (Yet internally the detailed language borrows from the organic fantasies of Paolo Soleri and Frank Lloyd Wright, i.e. a link was made between decorative expression and readings from Darcy Thompson's studies of organisms and structures in *Growth and Form*.) The 60s development of architectural ideas based on space age high technology go beyond modernism — by developing the real and achieved technologies of 20th-century America rather than the intellectualisation of technology that went with European modernism.

Louis Kahn's masters' class project 1963, a cultural centre for an American city: whilst Bucky's technology explored the limits of our architecture where 'change is normal', Kahn sought to find the constants — the unchanging nature of our institutions and the form our buildings give to them. The two apparently opposite theses frequently converge due to their essentially fundamentalist thinking.

The centripetal character of Paul Davidoff's Choice Theories and Planning Advocacy seemed at the time as right (and wrong) as Kahn's narrow focusing simplifications. Planning work in Philadelphia high-lighted the grid and the system both as tyrants and as providers of opportunities for everyone (1962-64). If in architecture the dichotomy to be resolved is between mass production and identification with the particular (artefact, context etc) and with expressions of identity and ownership, then in planning there is to be resolved the dichotomy between the mass, the social system and the political control on the one hand, and the enfranchised 20th-century citizen whose expectations of freedom, choice and share in community benefits have been so dramatically raised. The interplay of opposing urban scales of general and particular, controlling system and response events, form the basis of several planning projects — urban squares in the U.S. gridiron city 1963, the design of traffic intersections and how their potential design variations can be extrapolated to become a new kind of city (1964). Housing competition entries in New York City (1964) and planning studies in Camden, New Jersey (1964-65) and Bath, England, continue the exploration of 'as found' urban systems and structures.

The technological utopianism of Cedric Price and Ehrenkrantz led to non-architectural solutions to the traditional problems of building as enclosure. The Modernists' view of architecture as the art of engineering appears limited by comparison. Concepts such as 'technology as non-visual backdrop' and 'appropriate technology' dominated late 60s schemes for 'universal sheds' and 'clip-kit' or 'plug-in' architecture. The former separated functionalism from form, the latter elevated bricolage and ad hoc. The Students' Hostel 1968 accepted that the ad hoc clip-kit service tower and the retention and conservation of six Victorian houses were one interrelated statement. The tower made the overall external conservation strategy possible; the students' furniture unit made the detailed internal tactics of conservation possible — all the rooms with widely variable doors, mouldings, windows, plan form, could accept the same piece of universal furniture.

1 Clifton Nurseries, Bayswater, 1979-80
2 Student thesis project for the Blackpool Climatron, 1961
3 Students' Hostel, bathroom tower, 1968, construction photo

4 Plan of Cultural Centre for an American City, student project 1963
5 Study of urban grids and squares, student project 1962-64

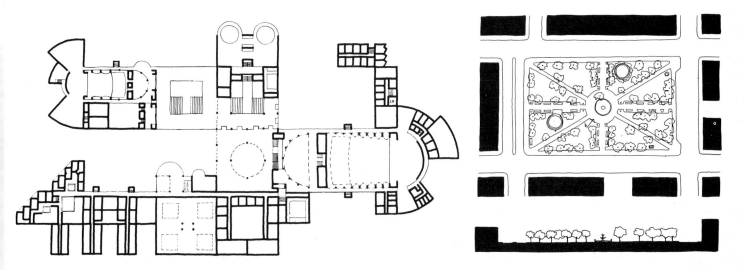

6 Oakwood 13 housing, a
framework for personal expression
(drawn by Andrew Holmes)

Mass-produced timber frame and mobile homes were more typical of the genuinely successful construction technologies of the 20th century as applied to house building than Corbusier's concrete or Mies' steel frame and all their imitators and successors. They developed from technologies that worked to obtain benefits of scale with more freedom of choice and opportunity for personal expression. Various mobile home and timber frame projects completed at this time included the *Sunday Times* Mobile House for isolated locations (1968).

Development of the city as fixed elements (movement grids, institutions, historic areas etc) and areas of opportunities led to various urban projects such as Aberdeen Centre 1974, Byrom Village and Manchester 1975. Many numerous conservation and rehabilitation projects were completed 1969-78 from boys' homes, individual and grouped residential, the Warehouse Theatre, Covent Garden, recording studios, offices and industrial buildings, shops and showrooms. Existing buildings are invariably refurbished because they are a resource but they additionally provide extraordinary opportunities for developing a design approach integrating contextualism, ad hocism and collage.

The natural progression from technology separated from architectural form led on the one hand to a greater freedom and relaxation in the use of technology, but on the other to increasing awareness of the emptiness of non-expressive, non-symbolic architecture. The flexible big factory shed with kit-of-parts cladding did not undo the progress made beyond modernism in the 60s (as the monumentalism and engineering-as-art object approach of late modernism/High-Tech did). However, the flexible shed lacked the formalisation of a language — ideally it was the language of pluralism but it readily became a tool for managements (rather than users) who 'expressed themselves' by maintaining cleanliness, efficiency and rather characterless anonymity. The Maunsel timber framed houses (1976-81), all on different sites but with the same underlying factory-made frame and inner skin, juxtaposed system and contextual expression. The Oakwood housing (1978-81) went further in developing links between expression and systems in that the timber frame system was specially designed for individual occupiers to create the surface (i.e. visibly perceived) architectural language.

An architecture solely derived from pluralism and flexibility lacks the formal character which a more structured and deliberately applied architectural programme brings. In the process the lessons from the 'Post-Modern' progress made by and subsequent to Louis Kahn and Bucky Fuller can be consolidated and built upon — but their rigorous and stripped fundamentalism left their students with a gap to be filled. Without doubt, Venturi built the essential bridges through his insight and demystification ('Main Street is almost all right'). By 1978 he summed up the final turn in the circle from modernism by defining architecture as 'shelter with decoration on it'. More than any other project, the collaboration with Charles Jencks on the house design which lasted several years led to developing and admitting into the repetoire a richer vocabulary. Through this working partnership the broadest view of 'inclusivity' became an integral part of subsequent work, which also built on the long apprenticeship in the various routes leading away from modernism (e.g. to take one random example, the building management methods utilised by High-Tech to invent new machine-made goodies proved to be translatable to decorative architecture: decoration, whether made by hand or machine, was subject to development and isolation as a 'sub-trade').

[1] Isaiah Berlin, *The Hedgehog And The Fox*, London 1953; see also Colin Rowe, *Collage City*, p. 92.

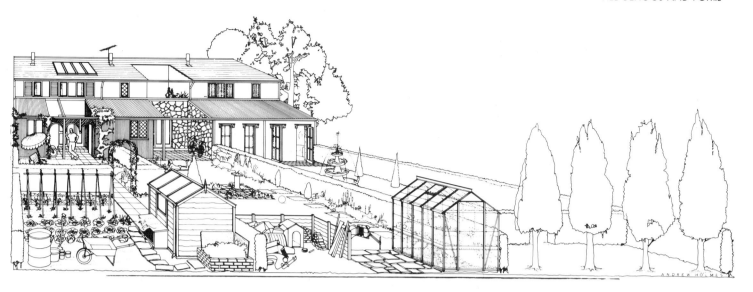

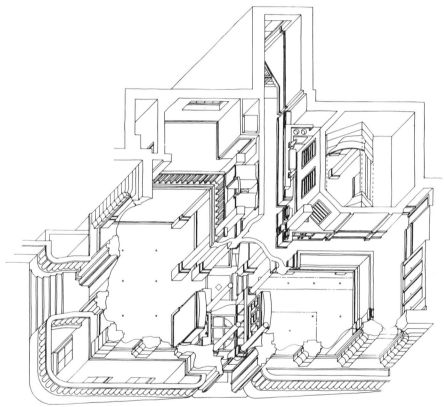

7 Crafts Council Gallery and
Information Centre, 1980-81,
axonometric
8 *Sunday Times* Mobile House
Project, 1968
9 Aberdeen Centre project, 1974

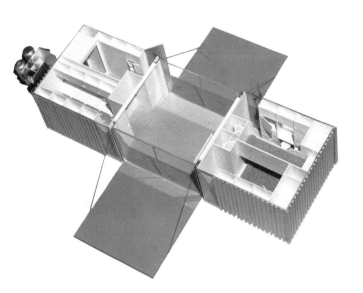

In the work since 1980 the human figure has been consciously acknowledged as a primary generator of architectural form. The measure of man not only gives scale but also lends proportion to plan and three dimensions. Anthropomorphic expression helps to structure the primary elements and the hierarchies of places within a building as well as being a more literal basis for collectively understood meanings of walls, windows, doors and so on. If in plan there is recognition of hearts, limbs and bodies, in elevation windows (as eyes), doors (as mouths), columns (as torsos) form part of total geometries where the symmetry and proportions of the human frame and its features provide a universally recognisable and reassuring code.

A Diagram after Francesco di Giorgio: the single figure in repose — static symmetrical organisation with simple hierarchies of plan and elevation.
Example: Eccentric building volume given 'other half' extension to make an axially placed facade.

1 The land available for Clifton's at Covent Garden ended at its edge along the prominent axis of King Street. The shop was built as a 'lean-to' against this boundary, leaving the maximum amount of site clear for a public garden.

2 The shop accommodation extrudes to the front facade and expresses itself in window and internal planting displays with open columns for visibility. The false half-facade screens rear car-parking with solid columns and open pediment for outdoor plant display. Three-column bays demarcate entrance on return facade.

B The single figure asymmetrical in movement — generated either internally by action within buildings' own organisation or externally by impinging demands of site (context, access, landform. . .).
Example: Axially organised structure and circulation, slipped in with shifted section and plan to provide ventilation and non-axial access.

3 First concept for Clifton's at Bayswater was a tree-shaped billboard gable and extruded to form a greenhouse: the compatibility of this form with the potential of the chosen building material (thermoplastic sheeting) led to the ultimate building form. The need for circulation between the building's two spaces (shop and greenhouse) led to the adoption of a central arcade whose arches were also the main structure over which the flexible cladding was draped.

4 The sealed environment of continuous sheets (within which it was difficult to make conventional window aperatures) led to shifting of section by adoption of continuous ventilation voids at ridge and plinth — on one side of the building only — through which air was drawn by passive solar methods. The plan was shifted to accommodate the main entry from the street and the main exit to the garden, each at right angles to the building's axis, and also diagonally opposed.
Example: Corner sites make for symmetries about hinge points which can be read from a variety of angles.

5 Flanks are extensions of street facades of the city block as well as folded-back arms of the building's own formal composition; hinge point is read in conjunction with opposing streets and corners as well as being a focus for the building.

6 Prominent corner building; historically a major entry to London forks at the site of Aldgate Pump to distribute traffic through the City. Convergence creates central focus of the building's main entrance which integrates pump monument into arcade. Boardroom 'crown' surveys and provides a beacon symbol to the City approach.

7 Comyn Ching corner building is one of six corner towers facing each other. The historic facades of the return flanks along Mercer Street and Monmouth Street reassemble their elements on the corner to provide a plinth and wings (arms) to the figure of the tower. The tower provides each floor of the building with a corner 'oval window' view of this piece of 18th-century town planning — Seven Dials.

8. Two back-to-back L-shaped buildings in Reading. Each is planned as wings or arms about a corner tower which houses corner entrance and vertical circulation routes as well as main rooms above. Eccentricities of site slope and unequal building sizes generate imbalance from what is a regularly shaped rectangular site.

C Grouped figurations: family portraits assembled in hierarchical format, like one body made from many. Each element is formally organised within itself.
Example: Add-on elements to large existing warehouse at Limehouse are like Lilliputians climbing over Gulliver; central entry hall, two side client rooms at ground level, two groups of dressing rooms at first floor and management suite at second floor are each framed as separate compositions in pyramidal forms and each level steps back from the one below.

9 Acrobatic balance of elements.

10 In plan the add-ons are placed on the half-bay module of the existing building's structural frame; each new element has a formal arrangement centralising on the existing columns.

11 The frames or portal elements identified.

12 The compositions within each frame identified.

D Urban formality results from almost accidental arrangement of 'family groups'; how groups link to and confront one another makes for uniqueness and quality of each urban settlement; over time historical layering results in collage effect.
Example: Vauxhall Bridge competition entry.

13 Extending the family groups to the limits of repetitiveness. Composite uses — housing, shops, offices — are each given their own view of the river and of one public open space, linked like beads on a necklace where each link is shifted 1° from the next to follow bend of river. Each of the four bands of building elements graduate in height away from the river bank to peer over the block in front.

14 Individual main blocks (offices and shopping) have bulk of the building accommodation crowned by public roof-top rooms (staff recreation/boardroom) and a masonry-arcaded plinth with formal entrances, each the central focus of the related public entrance place.

15 The minor blocks (houses and blocks of flats) have linear access and public space allocation; the flats' blocks have penthouse crown and plinth and paired front pavilions of large houses with roof-top living rooms.

16 The four layers are grouped and then linked to further groupings to make village elements within the overall city.

Example Four urban projects.

17 A building with quite separate contexts for main elevations at TV-am; to the rear the canal (north-facing) and to the south the road (south-facing) with main vehicle and pedestrian access. The two-acre site and variety of uses and existing buildings are exploited to fragment collective (corporate) images and build up elements so that complete building is a world of its own, expressed internally by gardens and pavilions with east-west-world-within-a-world symbolism.

18 One building type at Wood Green derived from planning the space outside the building is prime form determinant for the building itself, an essentially urban necessity. Six buildings which originate this way with varying boundary conditions and all within the same neighbourhood, stitch together run-down urban industrial area.

19 Alternative scheme for Mansion House; diagonal routes create triangular (flatiron) building elements. The facade and the points on the corners provide a variety of compositions from simple elements potentially far more dynamic and complex than conventional rectilinear planning.

20 Integrating new development with existing can mend old wounds and form the basis for recreating an urban centre at Hammersmith; almost an ecological activity — self-regeneration and growth over time is more important than resolving final building forms and uses now. Each successive development adds on to the city's historical base as a collage of set pieces.

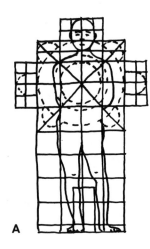

A

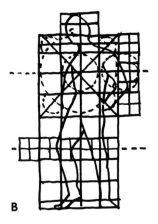

B

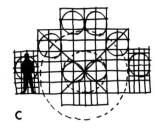

C

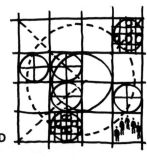

D

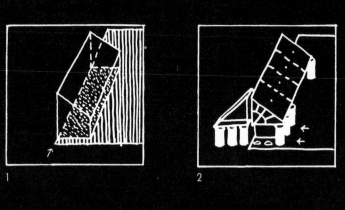

1

2

3

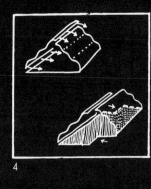

5

6

7

8

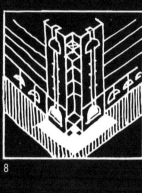

9

10

11

12

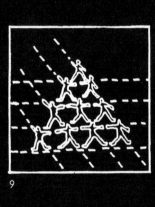

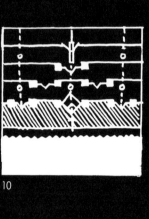

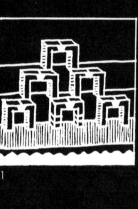

13

14

15

16

17

18

19

20

EARLY WORK

Early work 1965-80 in partnership with Nicholas T Grimshaw as Farrell/Grimshaw Partnership

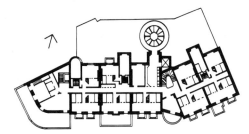

1 Typical floor plan

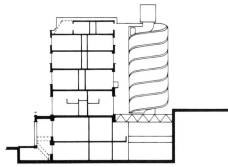

2 Cross section

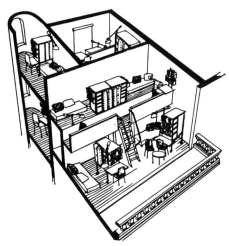

3 Gallery rooms on first floor

HOSTEL FOR OVERSEAS STUDENTS 1968

Paddington, London

Essentially a very low cost conversion of six large separate, dilapidated but historically important Victorian houses into a Church of England hostel and clubrooms for 200 students. All the spaces in the old buildings were converted into student rooms making for very efficient space utilization by placing all new bathrooms and kitchens in a service tower in the rear yards. The variety and character of the fine existing rooms was maximized by use of sleeping galleries at first floor, new attic rooms and a students' all purpose independent furniture trolley which meant that there was no fitted furniture in any of the rooms.

4 Rear view of hostel with service tower

5 Front view of historically 'listed' facade
6 Students' furniture trolley

7 Components of trolley

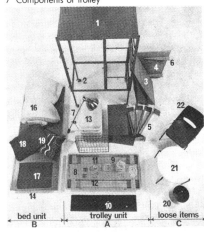

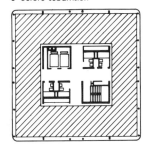

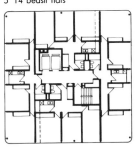

40 CO-OWNERSHIP FLATS 1970
Regent's Park, London

This low cost project began by attempting to tailor make 40 flats to the 40 owners who were collectively developing and living in the building. This approach was substituted for a highly flexible approach rather than a tight fit one as owners' needs and personal circumstances began to vary during design and construction. Cladding is in standard unpainted profiled aluminium sheeting; the spare concrete structure was designed by engineer, Tony Hunt.

1,2 External views from Park Road

3 Before subdivision   4 Flats as built   5 14 bedsit flats   6 2-4 bedroom flats

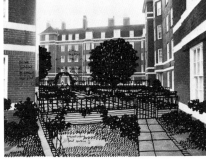

7
8
7, 8, 9, 10 Before and after photos and montages of the external spaces between buildings showing effect of landscaping around these essentially sound and well built dwellings

REHABILITATION STUDY OF 1,000 OLDER COUNCIL OWNED DWELLINGS 1975
Westminster, London

This study looked at eight existing housing estates and recommended a range of strategies which would restore these dwellings for a further 60 years' life and make them more pleasant, safe and popular. The external and internal environments were examined, as well as the ability of the homes to adapt and change as an essential part of the council's housing resource.

9
10

11 New bathrooms and kitchens zoned to ensure future flexibility in flat size and type

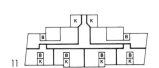

11

THE COLONNADES
1974-76
Bayswater, London

A three acre urban complex of 240 dwellings, offices, shopping, pub, library (unbuilt), garden square and underground car parking, won in a limited competition. Part of the housing was formed from retaining nine large characterful Victorian houses and applying a new layer of living rooms at the rear in the form of a vertical sandwich. Much of the rest of the housing was on the rooftops of the shopping precinct as linear patio houses of either 80' or 100' in length. The original mews was retained as was the ground level colonnade of the original houses which was extended round the new-build elements and encloses all public activities and maisonettes accessible from ground level.

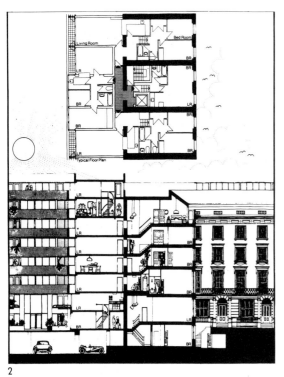

3

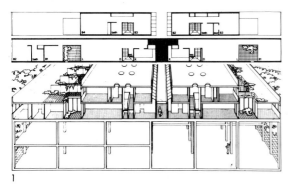

4

5

2

1 Plan and sectional perspective of residential units above shops/offices
2 Part plan and section through existing buildings showing new rear additions
3 Rear view of small houses along the line of the original mews
4 Terraced flats adjoining traditional dwellings and streets
5 Junction of existing restored houses and new flats with extension of colonnade

1

HOUSING SOCIETY SCHEMES 1972-80

A range of small scale low cost schemes were built, in backland and infill sites. Provision of all dwelling with ground level front doors and private gardens was an essential part of the brief. The housing was familiar and reassuring in character.

1 Family bungalows in brick and timber: Oxfordshire
2 Houses and old peoples' flats in render and timber: Watford
3 Timber framed terraced housing: Luton

2

3

FACTORY SCHEMES 1972-80

A wide range of industrial buildings as completed for occupation by companies like Citroën, Herman Miller, BMW and Digital as well as speculative buildings for new towns and developer clients. An expertise in lightweight cladding design, steel frame construction, and fast track construction contracts was developed. Peter Brett was the engineer for most of these projects.

4 Warehouse for Citröen: Runneymede
5 Factory and computer space for Digital Equipment Company: Reading
6 Detail drawing of ducts

4

5

6

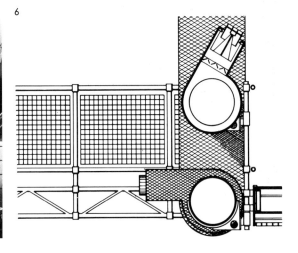

CLIFTON NURSERIES GREENHOUSE GARDEN CENTRE AND SHOP 1979-80

Bayswater, London

TF with Ken Allinson*, Page Ayres

This was the first of two buildings built by Clifton Nurseries as part of their policy of revitalising vacant city sites that were temporarily derelict. The client's concept was to take a short lease on the site and provide both a retail outlet for themselves and an environmental improvement for the community. Integral to the brief from Clifton Nurseries was the belief that the building should be more than just the usual cheap shed and glass lean-to; it should be something more representative of the visual pleasure of plants and gardens and it should be very much of the twentieth century, as representative of its day as the great Victorian greenhouses were of theirs.

An investigation of existing off-the-peg systems quickly revealed the necessity of starting the design from scratch. The building's form as it finally evolved derived from several concerns evident in this and other projects in the office. The axially-organised undulating form derived from the combination of the extruded plan and the use of large sheet materials recently made available for certain types of new technology agricultural greenhouses. Double-walled poly-carbonate sheet for cladding was used for the first time in Britain on this building and was considered appropriate as it combined high impact resistance, high thermal insulation and excellent light transmission and was relatively cheap.

The structure to which it is fixed is a demountable steel frame with a double-curved profile that both gracefully alludes to traditional garden conservatories and with its ·undulations gives strength and stiffness to the long lengths of narrow polycarbonate sheets without sagging. An M-shaped specially flexible sealing gasket in a polyurethene elastomer and a specially made PVC fixing button with a screw running down its centre ensure that the large thermal movements and bending stresses are accommodated without damage.

Environmental control to counteract large heat gains in summer and heat losses in winter is achieved by a combination of devices. Winter heat losses are controlled by the insulation of the polycarbonate; summer heat gain is controlled by blinds on the south elevations and by a self-ventilating and heat regulating system based on the principle of a solar chimney. A series of floor level and roof level vents and a suspended quilt under the southern roof of the arcade draw air naturally through the building and accelerate the ventilation by natural convection of the greenhouse, with the primary outlets formed by a vertical shift in the section alignment along the ridge.

The shift in plan form along the central axis accommodates two directions of entrance approach to the building and the solid gable-shaped cut-outs in the perimeter fence extend these axes beyond the building to the site boundaries.

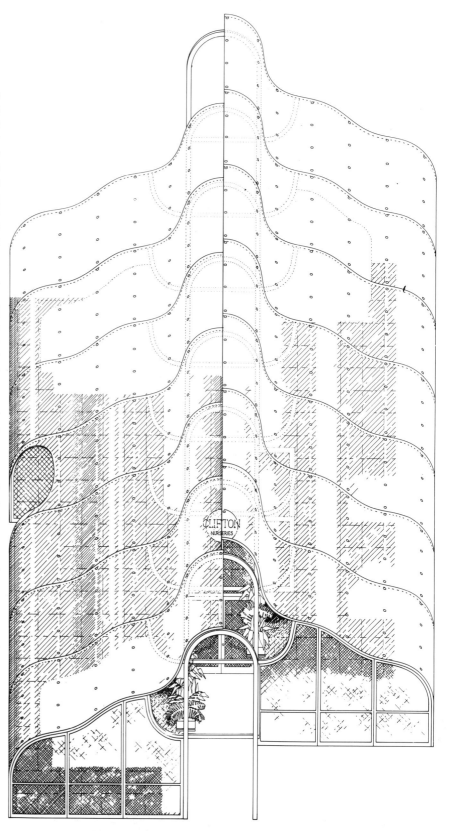

1 Axonometric

1 Axonometric

CLIFTON NURSERIES GARDEN SHOP AND PUBLIC PARK 1980-8
Covent Garden, London

TF with John Chatwin, Craig Downie*, Alan Morris, Richard Solomon

The garden shop in Covent Garden is the second temporary building designed for Clifton Nurseries on a short-lease central London site. This very prominent site is owned by the Covent Garden Opera House who intends to build a second auditorium here, but in the meantime it was vacant and an eyesore. The architectural response was to combine a formal solution which took its cues from the streets and buildings of surrounding Covent Garden with the continuing interest of the Partnership in the expressive qualities of new technology, particularly when applied to lightweight demountable structures. Given the location of the building — terminating a major street flanking the market buildings — and the formality of the surrounding street patterns, it was decided to align the building centrally on the axis of King Street. The available land did not extend symmetrically about this axis but permission was obtained for the facade to be extended along a narrow strip on the other side of the axis as a pure screen, which completed the symmetry and hid the car parking land behind. The problem of creating a facade and a building of appropriate scale and appearance for this historic context was resolved by adopting a classical portico, based on the precedent of the nearby numerous porticos of the market buildings and of Inigo Jones' St. Paul's Church, and extending it in a 'temple' form to become the underlying image of the design.

The interpretation of this classical form in the architectural detail of the new building was at all times to remain relaxed and light-hearted. This adoption of 'classical' details and the introduction of modern technology went hand in hand and were combined with a certain irreverence for their sources. The portico facade is a framework split along its central axis, each side containing planting and light displays that change with the seasons. Indoor plants and flowers from the shop are incorporated into the glazed window half of the portico and outdoor plants are arranged on the open framework side. The open columns are for plants to grow inside, and all the columns have living plant swags. In this way the business purpose of the shop — marketing plants and flowers — reflects in live form, classical stone decorations (which in turn derived their forms from the seasonal foliage of plants.) On the long facade a 'rusticated' glass and timber wall, representing the heavy stone side walls of a temple occupies three of the four garden bays — but in a contradictory manner as only the 'joints' are solid (as window frames) — the 'stone' element being replaced by glass windows to display the shop interior. A largely glazed non-rusticated shopfront turns the corner below the pediment and occupies the fourth entrance bay in the manner of a temple stoa.

The roof of the building is fabricated from Teflon-coated glass fibre, the first instance of the use of this material in Britain.

29

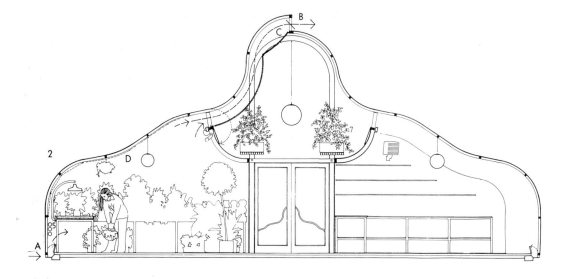

2

KEY

A   Vent air inlets
B   Vent air exhaust through louvre
C   Solar chimney formed by
    suspended quilt
D   Shading blinds

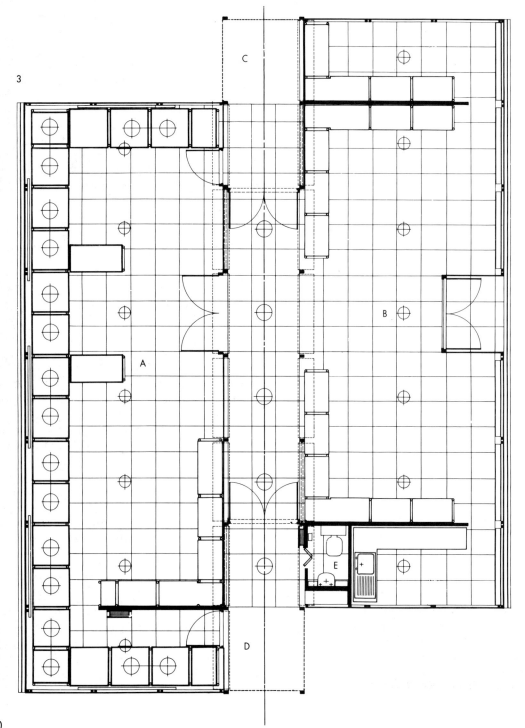

3

2 Section

3 Plan. The building in plan consists
of a central arcade through which
customers pass to enter the nursery
proper, with the shop on the north
side and the greenhouse on the
south

4 Exterior of entrance side at night.
Columned internal illumination and
the refraction of light on the webs
separating the twin walls of the
polycarbonate sheet give the
building a shimmering night-time
presence

5 Interior of greenhouse

6 Interior of central arcade

KEY

A   Greenhouse
B   Shop
C   Arcade
D   To garden
E   WC

4
5

6

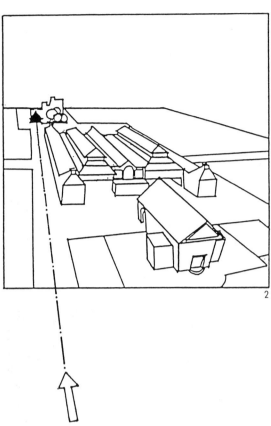

3 Site Plan
A St Paul's Church (Inigo Jones)
B Restored market buildings
C New garden shop and public Park

4 Cross section
A Tensional buttons give rigidity to:
B The fabric roof
C Side wall clad in profiled metal

5 Plan
A False half trompe l'oeil
B Main entrance from public park
and outdoor sales area
C Shop sales area
D Stores and toilets etc
E Service access

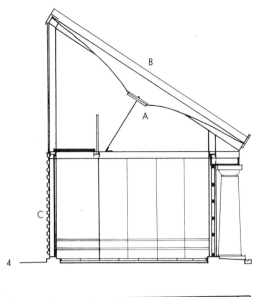

2 Although not occupying the full site needed, by means of a false half trompe l'oeil the building sits squarely on the axis of King Street, in an area unusually (for London) full of set pieces of formal town planning

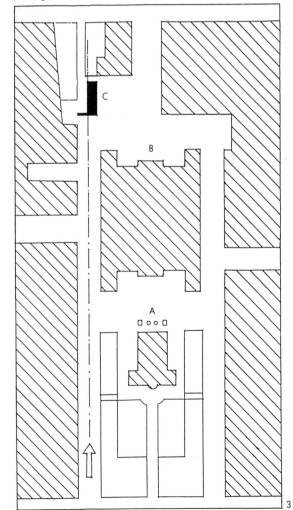

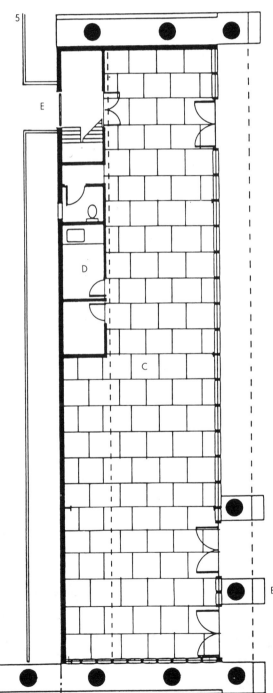

6 Front portico on axis of King Street

7 Exterior view at night. Illumination of the building at night was carefully considered. The translucency of the fabric roof provides an excellent diffuser for internal lighting and from the outside the roof in darkness adopts an appearance not unlike a large lampshade, with the tension buttons to each bay expressed strongly and surrounded by a blended variance of shadows. The front pediment is fully lit from floodlights positioned centrally at the base of the fan design and the capitals and lettered triglyph are internally lit

8 Side view from Public Park showing fabric roof with tension buttons and 'rusticated' arrangement of window mullions to glazed wall of garden shop

Page 34
CLIFTON NURSERIES BAYSWATER

7 Clifton's Bayswater. Exterior view from the garden centre side

Page 35
CLIFTON NURSERIES
COVENT GARDEN

9 Detail of trompe l'oeil screen

10 View down King Street

11 Night view

12 Clifton's Covent Garden. Exterior view from inside the restored Piazza buildings

6

7

8

7

9

10

11

12

LOW COST TIMBER FRAME HOUSING 1974-81

TF with John Chatwin, David Clarke*, Ray Bryant*, Joe Foges*, Nicholas Rank*,, Ken Allinson*, John Petrarca* (* all project architects for one or more schemes)

A. Seven small infill schemes for Maunsel Housing Society

The commission was to design, concurrently, seven housing schemes comprising over 200 houses, although several of the individual schemes were for less than ten dwellings. Dwelling types were family houses with gardens or family maisonettes over a lower ground storey planned as a separate flat so that each dwelling had easy access to its own private garden and front door to the street. A narrow party wall width of 3.6 metres was chosen to give maximum potential for individual street frontage; and the simple repetitive plan form which was developed proved to be very adaptable to the different site constraints and family use – much in the manner of the London Victorian terraced house.

Government finance was secured for a single 'serial' contract with a major timber frame manufacturer to supply and erect the entire superstructure, roof, windows and weathering for all schemes. Each project was then built under the overall control of a small local contractor who provided the management continuity and undertook those initial site works and final internal and external finishing elements appropriate for each site. In this way the quality control and economics of factory-produced repetitive timber frame construction was combined with the ability to respond to each local context.

B. 200 houses for Warrington New Town

The commission in 1978 by Warrington New Town Development Corporation to undertake the design of two large adjacent housing sites in Oakwood presented the opportunity to explore further these two concepts of standardisation of construction and individuality of context and personal expression.

The site access lanes run north-south, giving good orientation and terminating at the retained woodland edge in a row of bollards, and continue as footpaths through to the adjacent linear park. Each lane contains no more than 35 houses; each has its own front garden and front gate.

Standardised timber frame techniques were again used to produce economies of construction time and cost; however, rather than the simple repetitive plans of the Maunsel schemes, a concept of the 'universal core' (the main service, circulation, and living spaces of the house) was developed. This core was common to all house types whose variation in size and character was achieved by the addition of extensions in defined zones at the front and rear of each house so that – both physically and by the adoption of relaxed, traditionally decorative suburban elements of trellis, porch, store and patio – maximum encouragement was given to tenants to extend, adapt, and decorate their own house.

1 Red tile hanging and timber cladding at Luton

2 Rear of (1) above
4 Face balcony: Romford

3 Blue tile cladding: Luton
5 Brick cladding: Isleworth

6 Stages 1,2,3 — Local contractor does sitework and erects foundations and brickbase
Stages 4,5, — Factory made timber frame elements erected by
specialist
Stage 6 — Local contractor finishes off cladding and landscaping

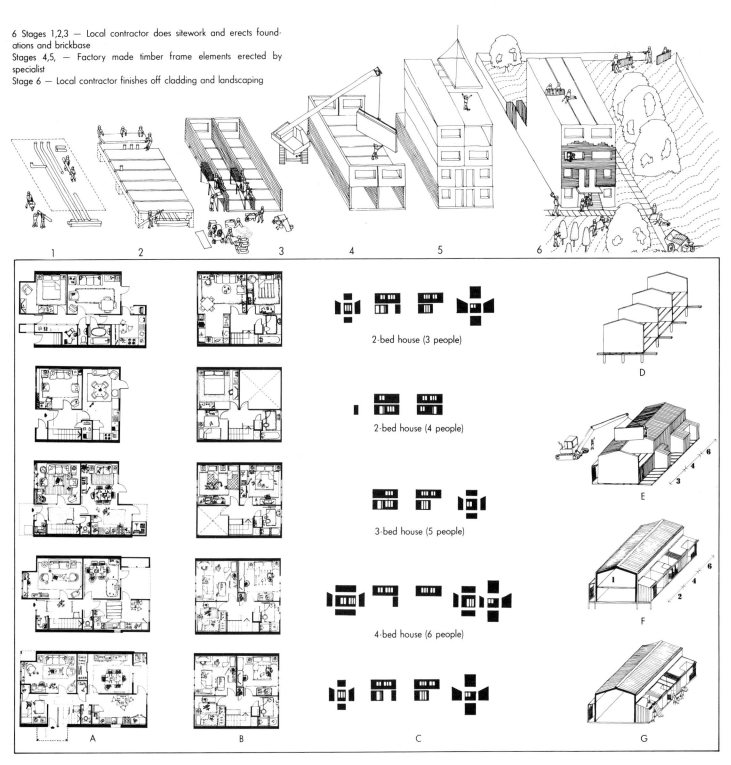

2-bed house (3 people)

2-bed house (4 people)

3-bed house (5 people)

4-bed house (6 people)

A   B   C   D

E

F

G

7 Different house plans (A+B) result
from adding variable timber panel
add-ons (column C) to central
masonry core (D) to make range of
house types in single terrace (E).
Later on management can vary
house types (F) or tenants do their
own add-ons (G)

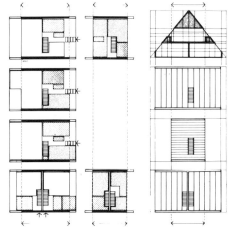

8,9 Oakwood 18: houses
developed the core and add-on
theme in a bungalow form where
all bedrooms were in the roof
space

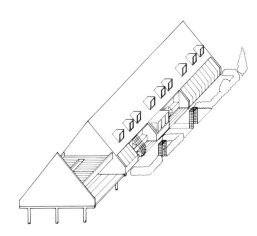

11 Front elevation of perimeter terraces of housing

12 Flats and maisonette front entrances
14 Grouped old peoples' houses

13 Typical lane with flats in distance
15 Front porches with decorated doors and trellis

16 View of the housing edge from perimeter footpath; low rise bungalows were adopted throughout this project

17 Factory prefabricated timber frame construction – showing components of one house

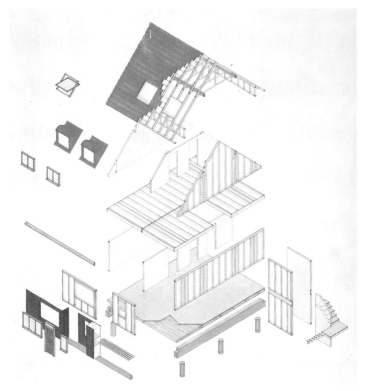

18,19 Typical views down OW 18 Lanes

URBAN INFILL FACTORIES 1979-81

Wood Green, London

for Samuel Properties in conjunction with Plessey Pension Fund and the London Borough of Haringey

TF with John Chatwin, Simon Hudspith, Peter Tigg, John Petrarca*, Geoff Warn

The commission for six factory units at Wood Green in North London was won in a developers' limited competition. A strategy of combining renovation and piecemeal re-development was adopted by the borough and the most run-down and least reusable existing properties were cleared to create six sites. These were developed by Samuel Properties as a single scheme of speculative industrial units each ranging in size from 400m² to 2,000m² with considerable flexibility for subdivision into different factory sizes.

A common solution was developed and adapted for each site where each building was built up to its site boundaries, whatever the plan profile, around partially enclosed courts. One of the characteristics of urban planning is that the design of open space becomes as critical as the design of the buildings themselves; at Wood Green each courtyard was a tightly designed formal arrangement of the turning circles and unloading positions of large vehicles, the car-parking of staff and visitors and the access and entry points of all vehicles and pedestrians.

The external walls at the boundaries of each site are constructed as a hard wall to enclose and protect and are in banded brickwork. The walls facing into the courtyards are constructed of a proprietary wall system with reflective glazing sealed in neoprene. The wide range of functions behind the factories' glass walls are partly hidden by the reflectivity of the glass and the use of this material in an enclosing ribbon wall makes the inside of each courtyard a sparkling, visually intensive area compared with the soft-coloured evenness of the outside brick walls — analogous in concept to a geode. These courtyard walls, in order to comply with thermal insulation regulations, have their mandatory element of required insulation in the form of set pieces of four square black opaque 'windows', a contra-dictory image reinforced by stripping the neoprene gaskets away around the black zones to reveal shiny aluminium window 'frames'. The courtyard glazing turns the corner at mid-span with silicon butt joints, and it steps back and up around the corner to the roof articulating the distinction between courtyard glazing and exterior brickwork whilst visually stitching the two together; it also provides visual contact between the mezzanine offices and the outside street.

Goods access is through a pair of double-height doors centrally positioned below the offices which extend at mezzanine level around the glazed courtyard walls. The location of stairs and toilets is fixed but their careful location between the office and industrial zones allows for flexibility in use. All the elements in the curtain walling are interchangeable and arranged within a square grid — a geometry which is repeated on free-standing elements such as gates, barriers and signs.

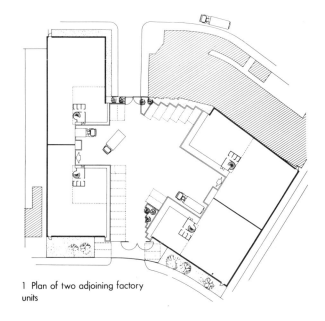

1 Plan of two adjoining factory units

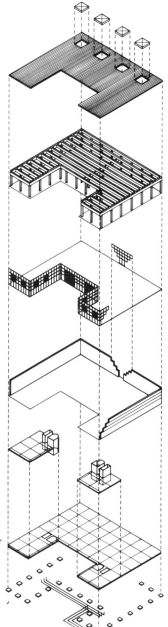

2a) Roof covering and rooflights

2b) Steel frame structure

2c) Internal flexible glass cladding to courtyard

2d) Exterior perimeter brick wall and service/access cores

2e) Concrete foundations and floor slab

3 Six courtyard factory units on
differing sites but in the same
neighbourhood

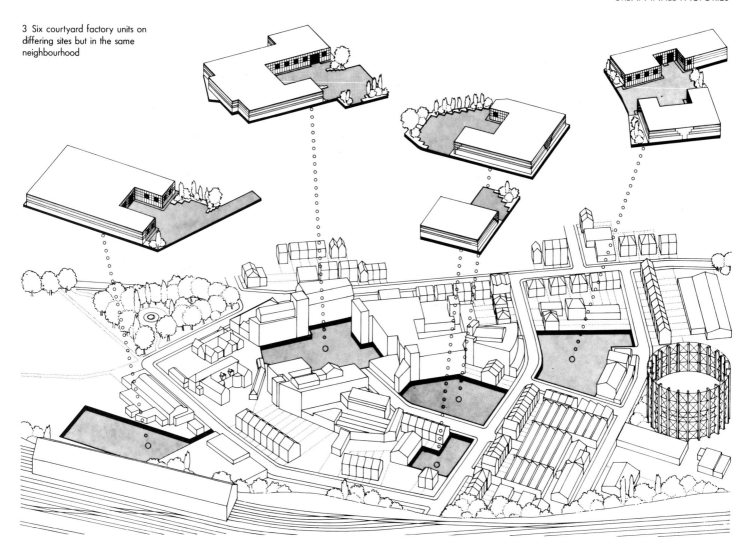

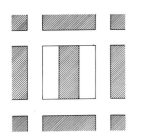

4a) Isolated building with no
response to context

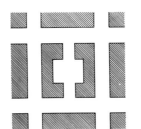

4b) Courtyard becomes the form
determinant

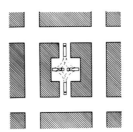

4c) Vehicle movement geometry
establishes configuration

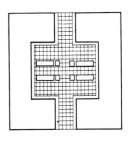

4d) Four factories serviced from
one courtyard

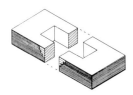

5a) Two buildings

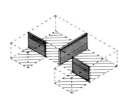

5b) Internal subdivision to two units

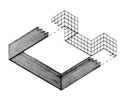

5c) Two wall types

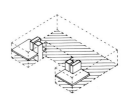

5d) Two cores

6 Perimeter banded brick wall interrupted by upper level windows and ground floor doors
7 Perimeter wall meets courtyard opening

8 Gates, glazing and brickwork junction

9 Two factory entry doors flanked by office/admin. wings
10 Mirror glass wall with black glass insets, louvre panels and steel vehicle barriers

11 Column of vent grills and cable tracks
13 Office staircase

12 Interior before occupation

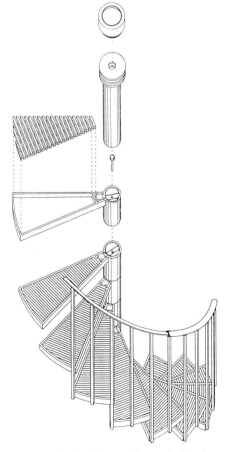

14 The spiral staircase is a radical modification of a standard product with inset treads made from shower matting

15 View from adjacent street
17 Specially developed neoprene gaskets for brickwork/glass junction and for timber door insets

16 Courtyard glazing junction

18 Cladding section

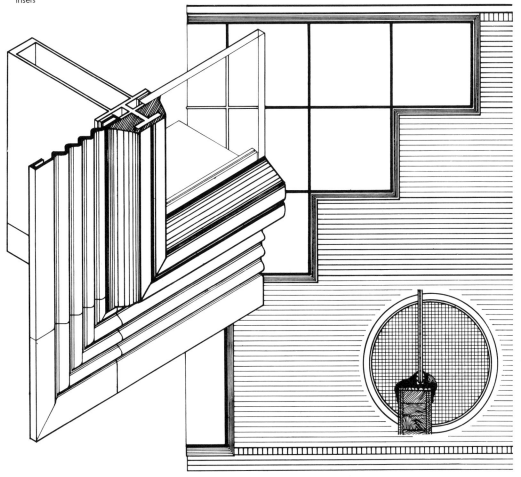

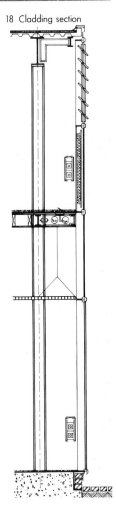

ARCHITECT'S OWN OFFICES
1980-81
Marylebone, London

TF* with Joe Foges, Simon Hudspith, John Petrarca, Doug Streeter, Simon Sturgis

The office is arranged around a central aisle flanked by a colonnade of six columns that provide incidents and define sequentially differentiated spaces and axes in their different ways. The centre of the main axis is located in the entrance area between a real column and its mirrored reflection, a *trompe l'oeil* necessitated by irregularities in plan and shortage of space.

The columns are not just formal and decorative, since they each rest on and define the location of essential space-consuming objects. The first pair of columns are hollow and are linked to the heating system, transmitting heat from ceiling ducts down to floor level. Central filing cabinets are located below the next pair, with power and telephone supplies being transmitted down the columns to all adjoining work spaces. Filing cabinets are positioned below the fifth and sixth columns. The actual work spaces are a series of rooms, defined by the columns, and a series of additional space functions are given identity by the colonnade. Thus, the staircase leading to further offices on the first floor, the walls to the kitchen and workshop area, and the secretaries' work space are all constructed from 'stone' coursed timber partitions within the column bays.

Other simple devices run continuously through the offices and serve to both dramatise special visual incidents and to impart a strong sense of unity to the general areas. The three-part cornice serves such a function, running along

(continued on page 48)

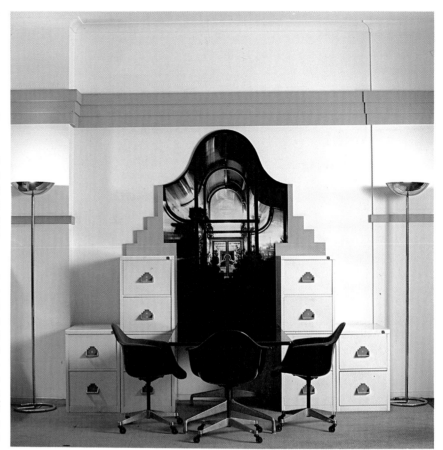

1 Reception area seating and reuse of existing filing cabinets as set piece
3 Central aisle with light columns electrical wiring ways and filing cabinet plinths

2 Axonometric of office space

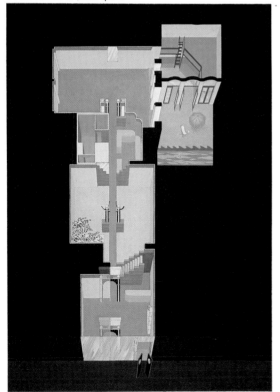

CRAFTS COUNCIL GALLERY AND INFORMATION CENTRE
1980-81
Waterloo Place, London

TF with John Chatwin, Joe Foges, John Langley*, Clive Wilkinson

The new gallery and information centre for the Crafts Council was built as both a conversion and an extension to their existing premises. Having acquired the lease of the basement, ground and mezzanine of the adjacent building, their requirement was for a new gallery space capable of subdivision into three separate areas as well as for a slide index, information and public coffee area; and for attendant office, storage, workshop and conference facilities.

The newly acquired building had a ground floor level two feet above the Craft Council's existing gallery but the mezzanine areas of both premises were on the same level. By repositioning the main entrance between the premises and lowering the level of the new entrance door and reception area, it was possible to form a new entry ramp (which provides easy wheelchair access around the entire ground floor). This ramp generates the main architectural strategy of the building — the creation of a central circulation axis from entrance to stair crossed by a cranked minor axis which runs through the two major gallery spaces. The entrance axis orientates the public on the gallery floor and also leads them through this area and the reception and sales area to the staircase which leads up to the mezzanine information centre.

1 Reference alcove, first floor, with reused slide index cabinets (cf Architect's Own Offices, 1)
2 Reception areas and front door

3 Axonometric of the three ground floor galleries

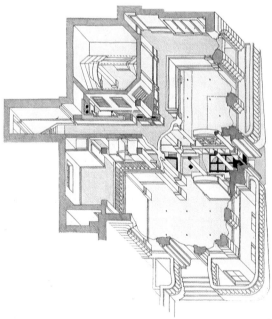

5

6

4 Partners' meeting room with office library in gallery above

the entire perimeter of the office, stopping only to emphasise the distinctness of elements such as windows. Elsewhere it is incorporated with the colonnade columns and used on its own along the ceiling to define the secretarial work spaces.

The inherited screen-based Herman Miller furniture system was retained and re-used in a way which contradicts its Bureaulandshaft origins. The furniture was pushed to the perimeter of each room off the central aisle to make maximum use of available natural light. Necessary adjuncts in an architects' office are carefully incorporated within the furniture layout; for example, vertical plan chests are aligned on the main axis at the end of screened work spaces and given identity and unity by being topped with 'volutes' incorporating lights and cutting surfaces.

Towards the rear where a mirror creates the illusion of a continuing colonnade a side axis leads to the partners' office. This double-height room has a small mezzanine of meccano construction from industrial Dexion decked in plastic 'high tech' flowers. The office library is on the mezzanine, and below it the two partners sit on either side of a central meeting space. Panels from the 1980 Venice Biennale which exhibited the Partnership's work cover the walls and provide an appropriate 'wallpaper' background to the colourful original 1930s' domestic Lloyd loom chairs. The partners' office leads directly to a small courtyard lightheartedly decked out to resemble a beach, complete with canvas windbreak, lifebelt, sand, waves, seascape and outdoor furniture. Here, in the centre of London the office can without sand in its sandwiches enjoy an hour on the beach in its lunch break.

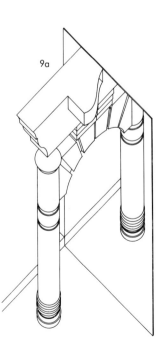
9a

9b

9a,b Front pair of columns with mirror/arch trompe l'oeil and heating ducts within columns

7

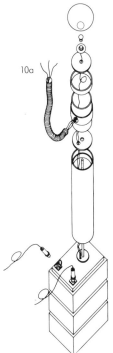

8

11 Central aisle with trompe l'oeil arch and main staircase

(Crafts Council continued from page 47)

5, 6, 7, 8 Various work spaces in the office

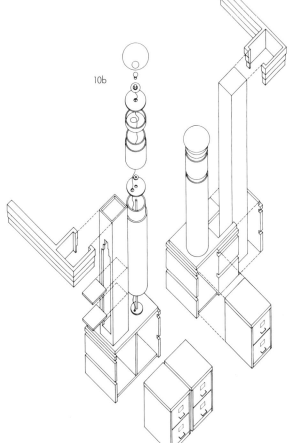

10a One of the central pair of columns with wiring routes and filing cabinet plinth

10b Rear columns over plinth filing cabinets, paired with one existing real square column and one storage column

The detailed architectural problem was identified as one of creating an internal identity whilst at the same time finding a visual language that reconciled the differing characteristics of the two historically listed, vaguely classical Victorian interiors and provide a neutral background for the display of objects in the gallery spaces. The more idiosyncratic of the original mouldings and decorations were simplified by the addition of new larger scale mouldings; and additional blank white wall spaces have been created wherever possible above a common skirting line, which becomes a plinth to the counter, bookshelf, and other elements in the lower floor areas. Recessed tracks for spotlights have been incorporated into additions to the existing ceiling modelling and subdued patterning in the new timber flooring acts with these modified ceilings to define sub-spaces within the two single-storey galleries. The taller space of the original gallery has had its suspended ceiling removed — revealing a splendid and ornate strap moulded plaster ceiling, and the new gallery lighting is suspended below on two trussed lighting gantries. New fibrous plaster columns flank the principal axes; a storage unit, a reception desk and bookshelves define the entrance reception/sales area, and the geometry of the new inset coloured linoleum flooring is designed to respond to the various activities along its length.

At mezzanine level the removal of part of the wall dividing the two mezzanines has allowed the introduction of a set of slide display cases in arched study carrels to create views back down into the galleries below. A long profiled coffee bar was designed with specially commissioned bar stools designed by Fred Baier.

4 Top end of new ramp, existing stair to mezzanine beyond

5 Reception area, with desk, bookshelves/display cabinet and fibrous plaster columns

6 Gallery Number One

7 Mezzanine Coffee Bar

8 Gallery Number Three

PRIVATE HOUSE 1978-81
First Phase London

Terry Farrell and Charles Jencks

With John Chatwin, Simon Hudspith, Maggie Keswick, David Quigley*, Richard Solomon and Simon Sturgis*

Jencks and Farrell worked together with others on this conversion of the Jencks family house in London. It has evolved over many years, but the initial phase of renovation, shown here, was largely designed by Jencks and Farrell. The existing nineteenth-century house has had a curved-roofed study and conservatories added to it, but otherwise the basic grammar of the exterior has been kept or marginally transformed. The interior has been extensively restructured around a new circular staircase, placed in the centre, which acts as the focus of movement. A structural cylinder, holding not only itself but also the two adjacent walls, it has been cut at various points to allow light and surprising cross-views, sometimes uniting four rooms in a single vista. The new timber roof and ceiling structures were developed in a complex symbolic and spatial manner. The rear conservatories, with amplified sash windows, link the interior spaces with terraces and garden: thus slots of space carry through from the street side of the house into nature.

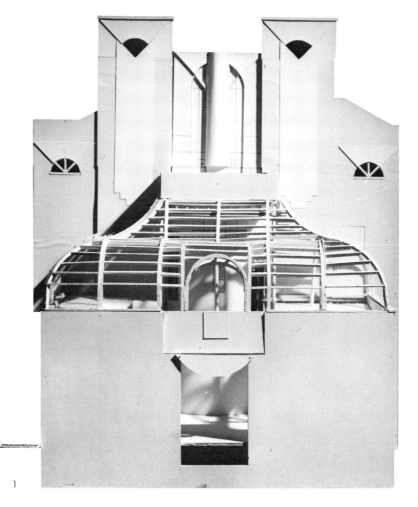

1

1-3 Study Annexe Model. The roof and stairwell structures, worked out with the engineer David French, show the interaction of symbolism and constructive logic. Five 'London Columns' were at this stage of design abstracted and used to order the side elevation; in the ceiling plan below this the sun rays radiate from the central staircase, the 'sunwell'.

4a-d Interior floor plans show the typical terace-house rhythm, ABBA, overlaid by the central staircase and outdoor balcony, two conservatories facing south, and a diagonal organisation of views.

5a Stair Tread — plan and three profiles tread with seven steps on front nosing.

5b Reflective ceiling plans show stairwell 'sun' radiating out and intersected by other geometries which underline the space below.

2

6 View of the stairwell face, the 'Jencksiana', layered construction, 'rays of the sun', 'clouds' and 'bookcase-skyscraper' — a mixed metaphor.

7 The Sun and Light Orders, made from Runtal radiators and sconces, frame the dining area and view over the garden. Overhead the diagonal structure of the sun's rays spread from the sunwell.

8 West elevation shows the tall chimney orders, two 'London Columns' setting the theme of duality which organises this facade. The curved 'Hildebrantian motif' of the roof will be complemented by two sculptural elements. The sun and face images organise the centre of the facade which is further emphasised by the dropped ornamental band.

9 The moonwell of two storeys, opposite the sunwell, has the window theme, which runs throughout the hosue, reflecting in the mirrors the crescent moons.

10 The sunwell brings light not only into the basement but to adjoining rooms; spatial interpenetration is combined with cut-through vistas.

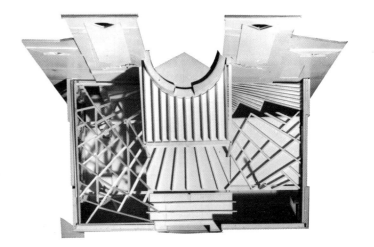

3

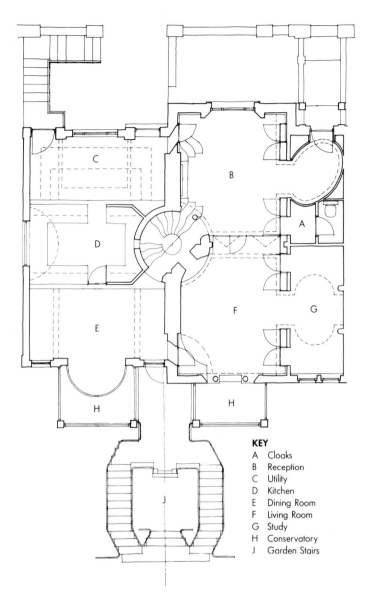

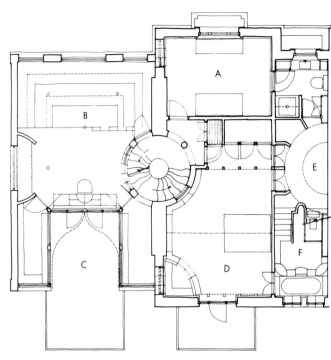

KEY
A Cloaks
B Reception
C Utility
D Kitchen
E Dining Room
F Living Room
G Study
H Conservatory
J Garden Stairs

KEY
A Guest Bedroom
B Study
C Terace
D Master Bedroom
E Dressing
F Bathroom

4a Ground Floor Plan

4b First Floor Plan

4c First Floor Plan

4d Second Floor Plan

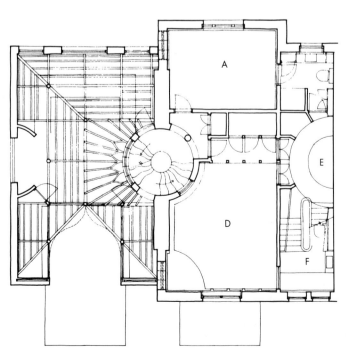

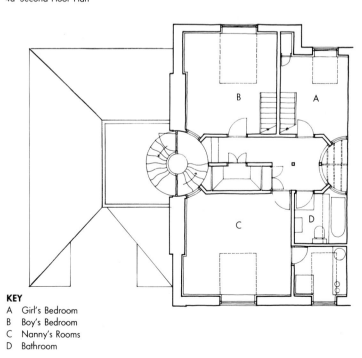

KEY
A Girl's Bedroom
B Boy's Bedroom
C Nanny's Rooms
D Bathroom

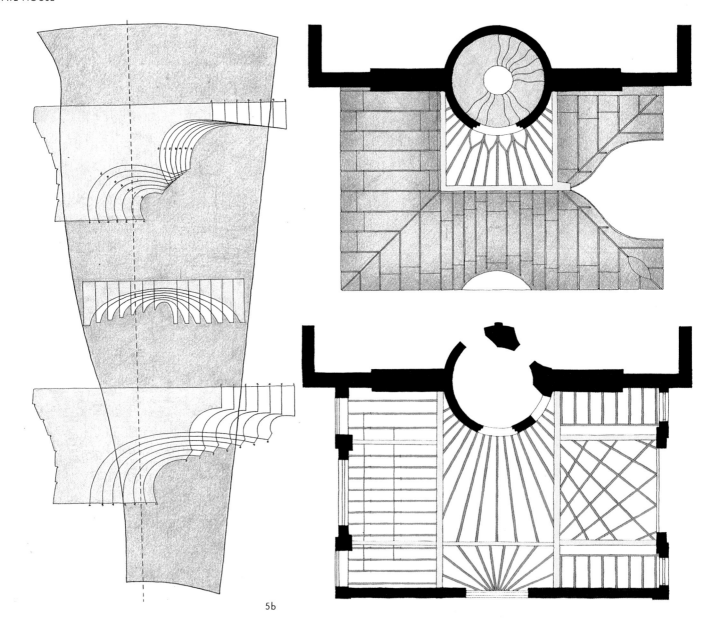

5a   5b

6   7

8

9

10

FESTIVAL EXHIBITION BUILDING 1982

Dingle, Liverpool
for the International Garden Festival 1984

TF with John Chatwin, Steve Ibbotson*, John Langley, Oliver Richards, Gary Young

This project was awarded second prize in a national competition organised by the Merseyside Development Corporation. The brief was for a large exhibition building to be converted after the one-year Festival concluded into a public recreation and leisure centre.

The design extends the thinking of the Alexandra Pavilion project; it is a fabric-covered steel-framed structure axially planned, with a large main hall and subsidiary adjacent spaces. The multiple cascading forms at the gable ends house smaller ancillary volumes, as well as reducing the scale of the building at ground level — particularly at the entrance points.

The single skin of PVC fabric would be increased to a double skin for the second stage, and for this a superior fabric with an increased life expectancy such as Teflon-coated glass fibre would be used. The drawings illustrate various colours and designs for the external envelope.

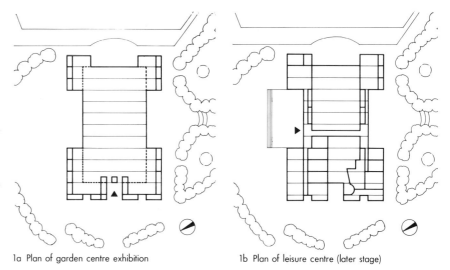

1a Plan of garden centre exhibition

1b Plan of leisure centre (later stage)

2 Axonometric of first stage building envelope

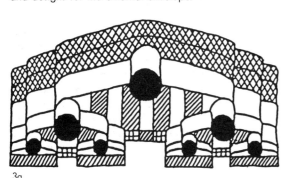

3a

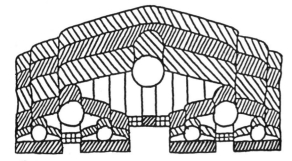

3b

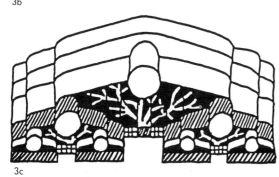

3c

3a,b,c Alternative designs and colour schemes for the external envelope

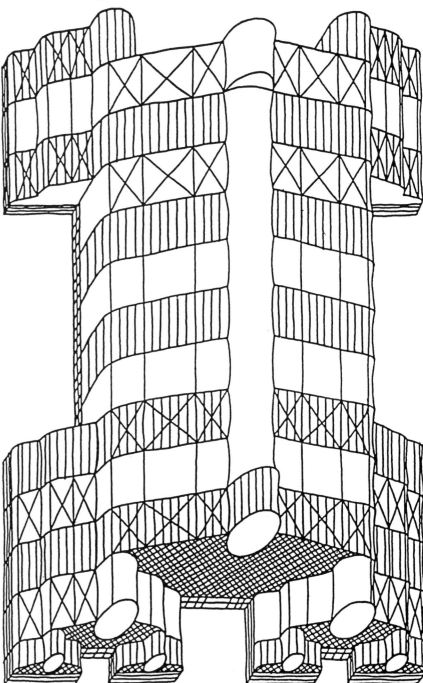

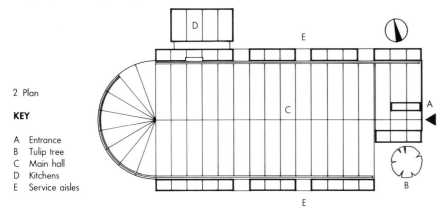

1 View from the existing building forecourt

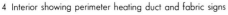

2 Plan

KEY

A Entrance
B Tulip tree
C Main hall
D Kitchens
E Service aisles

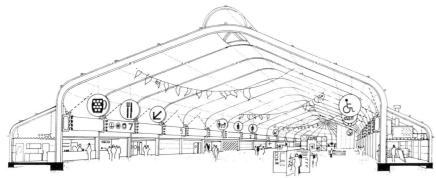

3 Cross section/perspective
4 Interior showing perimeter heating duct and fabric signs

ALEXANDRA PAVILION
1980-81

Haringey, London
for the London Borough of Haringey

*Designed in conjunction with Peter Rice and Ian Ritchie who developed the Shelterspan system and Dr. Peter Smith of the London Borough of Haringey
TF with John Chatwin, Michael Glass, Oliver Richards**

When the Victorian Alexandra Palace in North London was gutted by fire, the local authority owners decided to house exhibitions, concerts, sports events and conferences in a temporary structure until the original building was reconstructed. The commission for this structure was won in competition.

The completed building in effect is a radically adapted version of the standard Shelterspan system. This system is for an enclosing membrane of PVC-coated terylene woven fabric panels supported on a rigid structure of aluminium portal frames. The technique of fixing the fabric derives from sail technology and consists of a luff groove set on the structural member into which is slotted a bolt rope attached to the edge of the fabric panel. The fabric panels are tailored to double-curved patterns using welded seams. The stable double-curved form of the panels prevents wear and tear through flapping in the wind, whilst at the same time creating the attractive scalloped appearance.

The large 36 metre span required for this pavilion had to be achieved by substituting steel for the standard Shelterspan aluminium portal frames. The steel portals are clad on the upper and lower flanges with standard aluminium fabric retention grooves fixed with chromium-plated bolts and plastic separating membranes. External purlins and diagonal rod bracing provide longitudinal stability. With an uninterrupted clear space of 3,620m² the building, when built, was the largest double-skinned fabric structure in Europe.

The characteristic cascading appearance of the building derives from the internal organisation which consists of a large clear spanned hall bounded by side aisles of all ancillary spaces such as stores, kitchens, toilets, first aid rooms, bars and snack bars. At the entrance end the buildings' extruded section is extended along one side of its central axis only, to avoid an existing mature tulip tree and to provide a formal termination to the linear form.

The internal environmental conditions are regulated by the thermal insulation of the double fabric skin, by fan-assisted natural ventilation and by gas warm air heating ducted into the main space through a functional 'cornice' around the perimeter of the enclosure. The pavilion is designed to be demountable and can be easily unbolted and re-erected on another site.

The form of the building relates closely to the first Clifton Nurseries building which also explored the formal resolution of an engineering structure in which a long length of 'soft' material was fitted into a steel framework, like rolls of fabric along curved ladders. The internal uplighters in the Alexandra Pavilion transform the building into an enormous lampshade at night, giving the building a dramatic luminous solidity.

5 Internal uplighters transform the building (at night) into a giant 'lampshade'
6 Entrance area of building at night

7 Rear view with existing Alexandra Palace

8 Entrance area, with stepped plan-form around existing mature tulip tree
9 Interior during windsurfing exhibition

10 Detail of entrance area

WATER TREATMENT CENTRE 1979-82

Reading, Berkshire
for Thames Water Authority

TF with John Chatwin, Andrew Cowan*, Michael Glass, John Letherland

This building was constructed as part of a new operations centre designed to deal with sewerage treatment and water supply for the Thames Water Authority, one of the largest water authorities in the world.

Apart from all the underground tanks and water treatment plant (part of a separate civil engineering contract) facilities were required in this building for workers who maintain other installations in the area; these included laboratories, cafeterias, stores, workshops, offices and a computer room. In addition, a centrally-placed visitors' centre was included to inform the public of the authorities' operations. The building straddles like a catamaran an enormous treatment tank set into the ground and containing several million gallons of water; weight and stability are provided by the above-ground building as the underground elements are made periodically unstable by the rising and falling water table, due to the proximity of the adjacent River Kennet. One metre of earth spread over the courtyards provides additional weight. Earth mounded for one metre up the wall externally to the top of the underground water tank reduces the effective height of the building on a visually sensitive open rural site and prevents possible damage to the cladding caused by operational vehicles.

Externally the building is clad in light blue glass which provides a low maintenance skin reflecting the colour of the sky. This blue colour and the cascading curved form of the central block alludes to water. The cladding grid responds to the requirements of different areas of the building. The rectangular grid (less expensive because there are fewer frame members and openings) covers the windowless single-storey stores which need large openings for deliveries. The smaller square grid encloses the two-storey accommodation which requires many small openings. The comparative low cost of the rectangular grid as opposed to the 'average' cost of the square grid produces a net saving; this is used to pay for the higher cost of the curved grids. Louvres on the southern end walls exclude solar gain.

Internally the planning provides for the two entirely separate usages by visitors and workers. Visitors approach along the central axial entry, through the main doors and into the ground floor exhibition area where the seating and the main door handles echo the Thames Water Authority's own symbol of gentle rising and falling waves. A central stair leads up to the full-width vaulted mezzanine gallery at the ends of which are, respectively, the platform for viewing the rest of the treatment works and the spiral staircase leading to the cavernous machinery hall in the underground structure. The staff entrances to the building are directly below these galleries' ends on each flank of the building. The colours internally contrast with the sky and water allusions of those externally and are more varied, earthlike and warmer.

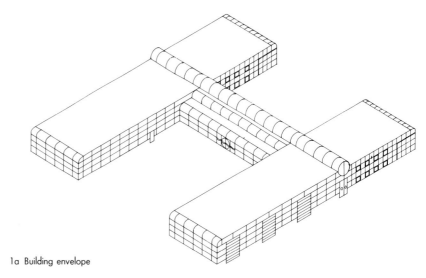

1a Building envelope

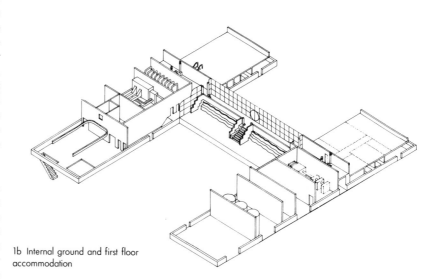

1b Internal ground and first floor accommodation

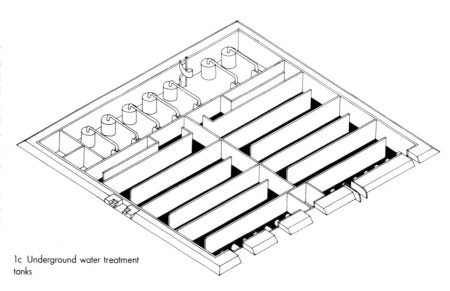

1c Underground water treatment tanks

2 Exterior with workshop wing in foreground

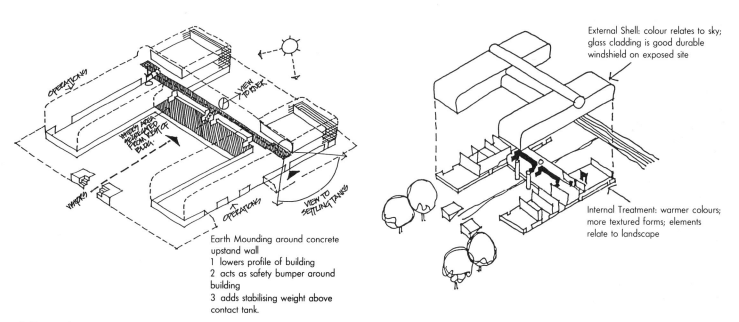

Earth Mounding around concrete
upstand wall
1 lowers profile of building
2 acts as safety bumper around
building
3 adds stabilising weight above
contact tank.

External Shell: colour relates to sky;
glass cladding is good durable
windshield on exposed site

Internal Treatment: warmer colours;
more textured forms; elements
relate to landscape

3 Concept diagrams
4 Main visitors' entrance to exhibition area: workshop wing on left, stores wing on right

5 Main visitors' entrance at night: side wings are in opaque blue glass

6 Visitors' viewing gallery looking down to main exhibition space

7 Interior of visitors viewing window at the end of gallery

8 Visitors' centre and exhibition space; stairs to gallery rise over 'wave' bench seats

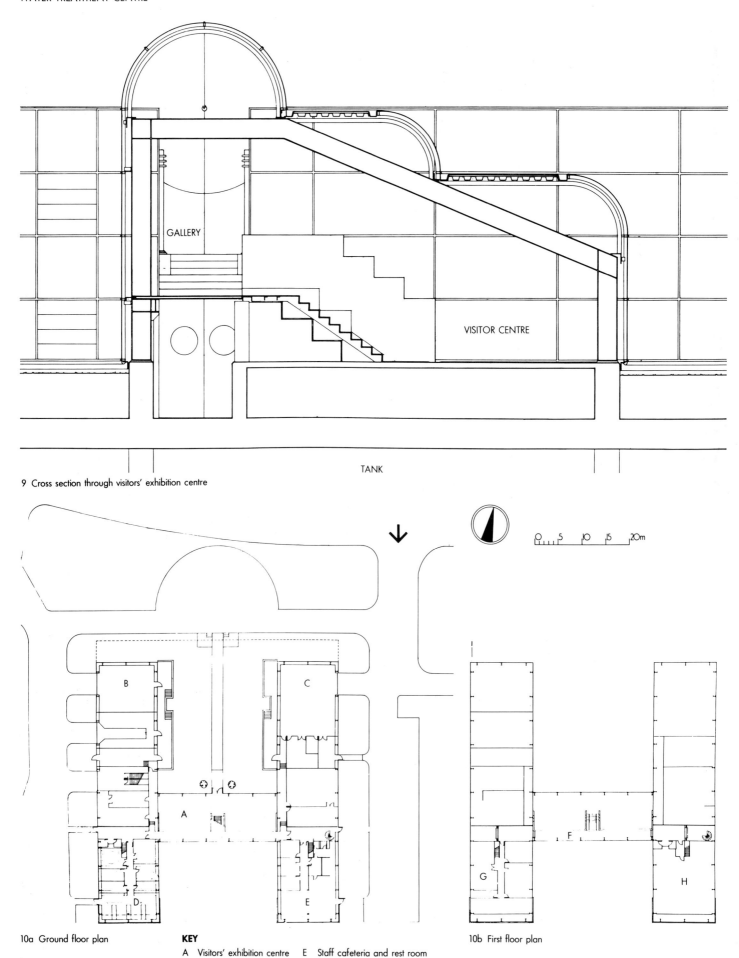

GALLERY

VISITOR CENTRE

TANK

9 Cross section through visitors' exhibition centre

0 5 10 15 20m

10a Ground floor plan

B
C
A
D
E

10b First floor plan

G
F
H

KEY

A   Visitors' exhibition centre
B   Stores wing
C   Workshop wing
D   Laboratories
E   Staff cafeteria and rest room
F   Visitors' viewing gallery
G   Offices
H   Expansion space

11 Stores wing in foreground, offices and laboratory wing in distance
12 Visitors' gallery viewing window from outside

13 Junction of reflective glass walls and opaque glass 'solid' cladding

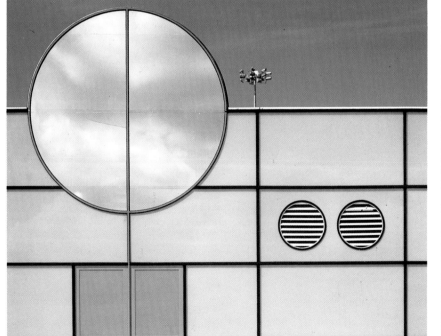

VAUXHALL CROSS NATIONAL COMPETITION 1982

Vauxhall Cross, London
for an urban complex for the developers, Arunbridge

TF with Laurence Bain, Michael Glass, Peter Jenkins, John Langley, Satish Patel, Oliver Richards, Gary Young*

This scheme for a site on the South Bank of the Thames at Vauxhall Bridge was one of the three winners selected by the assessors in a two-stage national competition. The final selection of the scheme to be built (which was not this scheme) was made by the developers, Arunbridge. The competition was initiated by the Minister for the Environment in an attempt to bring development to a site that had remained derelict for some thirty years. By promising to make the winning scheme the subject of a Special Development Order in Parliament (thus avoiding the normal planning procedures) and by increasing the plot ratio of 2.5:1, and the commercial to residential mix of 3:1 (as defined under the G.L.C. General Development Plan) to the more profitable levels of 3:1 and 4.7:1 respectively, the Minister made the scheme commercially very attractive.

The elements of the scheme are conceived as parts of a new village (London is more like a collection of villages than a city) and are disposed along a linear plan like beads on a necklace which have in parallel to each other and the river a central public pedestrian mall, a residential mews, a riverside walk and a business users' route on the roadside. These four routes are intersected at right angles by pedestrian routes progressing from the underground station, commercial and office areas through the site to the river walks.

The staggering of the plan also creates a series of pyramidal arrangements when viewed from across the river. This effect is increased by the careful positioning of office conference suites and residential penthouses, of related pedimental form and increasing size, along the buildings' roof tops. The addition of these functional but formally arranged elements to what are essentially straight-forward building blocks was intended to unify the overall composition and create a dramatic and recognisable silhouette by day and night (as the site is on the South Bank the buildings will be perceived against sunlit sky).

The main elements of the scheme each shift through an angle of 1° with respect to each other, thus following and emphasising the bend in the river. The smaller scale of the riverside residential buildings is continued into the office area by the use of a five-storey podium to the office blocks constructed of banded brick and stonework; this 'masonry' plinth encloses housing, office blocks, shopping, pubs and with its arcades, balconies, entrance porches and mixed variety and uses is perceived as a complex, familiar and traditionally constructed lower strata — the village world of the person moving at ground level. This podium also relates to, and incorporates, the existing listed Georgian brick building at the rear of this site. The office buildings rise as a separate strata above the plinths reflecting the light and the sky and are of glass in three reflective colours or tints, with mirrors for the surrounding smaller grid windows, green tint for the front blocks and blue tint for the rear blocks.

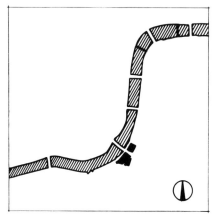

1 Location plan: Vauxhall, London

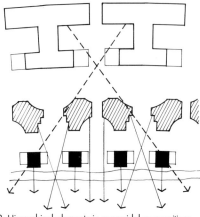

2 Hierarchical elements in pyramidal compositions

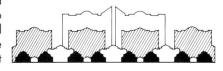

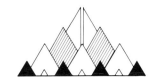

3 Arrangement of Blocks allows views to river

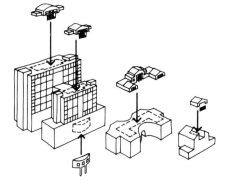

4 Each element of four bands of buildings is crowned by a major room

5 View of model from the east, Vauxhall Bridge in centre

6 Site plan

KEY
A Vauxhall Bridge
B New piers and landing stage (floating)
C Office entrance courts for pedestrians and vehicles
D Central pedestrian mall
E Residential access mews, pedestrians and vehicles
F Rear tall offices
G Front lower offices
H Rear residential in flats
I Front pavilion residential, houses and studios

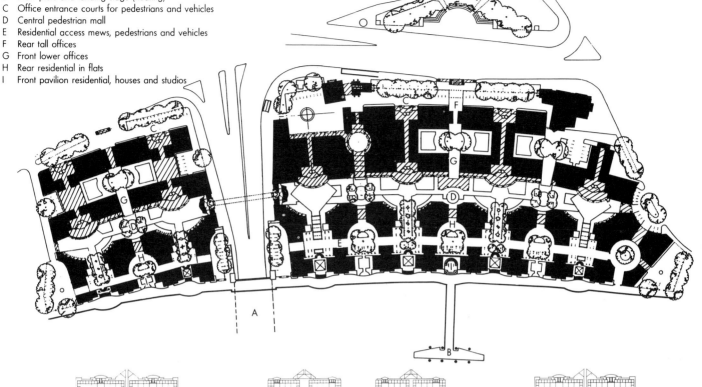

7 Full site elevation from south and north (river elevation)

8 View of model from the north, floating piers in foreground. In section the site is arranged with two blocks of housing at the front, and two blocks of offices to the rear, increasing in size from front to back to allow each a river view. In plan the building blocks are staggered and irregularly profiled to produce a variety of external spaces in size and shape and to maximise views from within the site to the river. These syncopated rhythms create a significantly richer and more complex geometry along the linear 'necklaces'

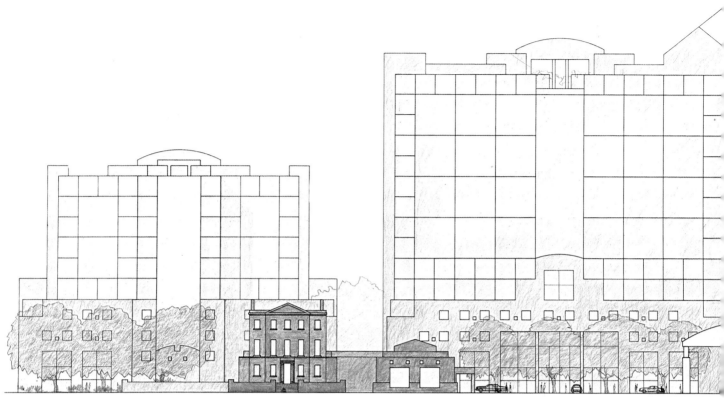

9 Rear elevation

10 River elevation

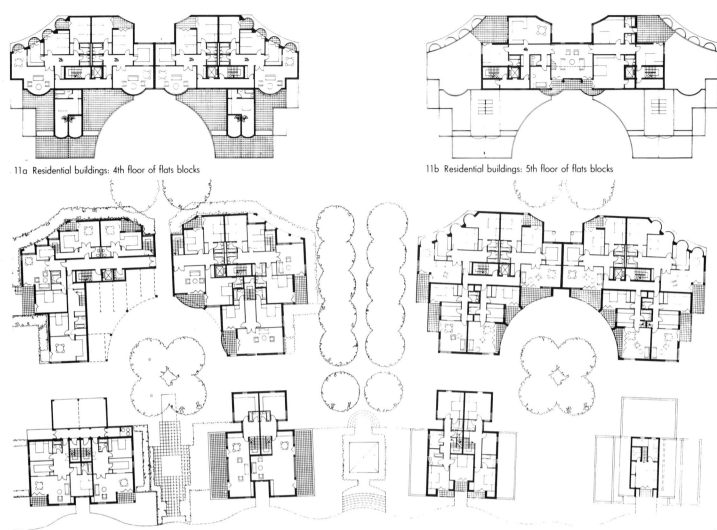

11a Residential buildings: 4th floor of flats blocks

11b Residential buildings: 5th floor of flats blocks

11c Residential buildings: ground floor and first floor of flats blocks and front pavilions with part of linear mews access route between

11d Residential buildings: 2nd floor flats and pavilion buildings

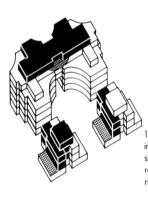

12a The residential buidings incorporate a large variety of unit sizes, e.g. 4-bedroom 'Palladian' rooftop penthouse, and 3-bedroom riverside maisonettes

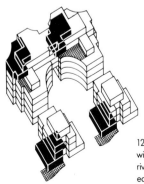

12b 2-bedroom penthouse units with main rooms and terrace facing river, 2-bedroom units on waters edge with garden

13 Study model to establish layered silhouettes

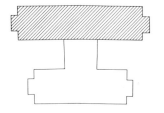
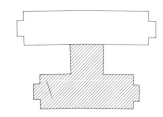
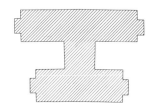

14 The office buildings by their shape and arrangement permit considerable flexibility of occupation

15a Office buildings: typical upper floor of offices (floors 6-11)

15b Office buildings: typical ground floor

16 Detail of glass cladding: part elevation and typical section at floor edge

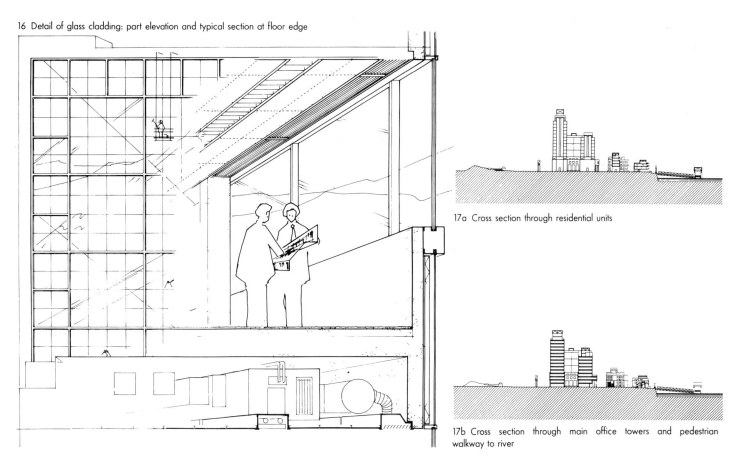

17a Cross section through residential units

17b Cross section through main office towers and pedestrian walkway to river

1 Atrium interior with transformed existing bridge within the Mediterranean Garden
2 Mediterranean 'Temple' bridge   3 'Zigural' central stair   4 Eastern 'Temple' Hospitality Room

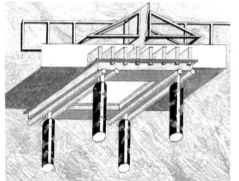 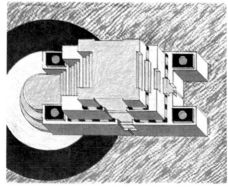 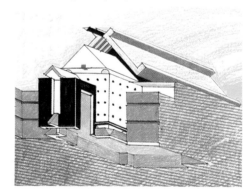

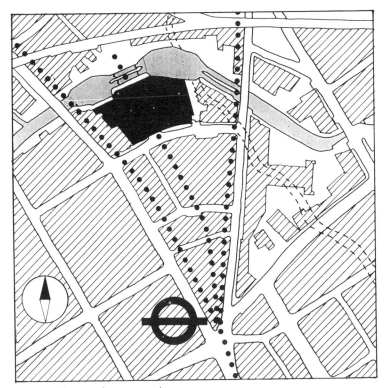

5 Location Plan: Camden Town, London

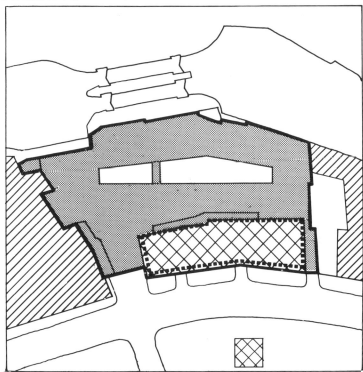

6 Site Plan: Building retained (in tone) new buildings (cross-hatched)

7 Aerial view of site

TELEVISION BROADCASTING CENTRE 1981-82

Camden Lock, London
for TV-am

TF with Joe Foges*, Neil Bennett, Simon Sturgis, Clive Wilkinson, Caroline Lwin, Doug Smith, Satish Patel, Peter Jenkins, John Letherland, Craig Downie, Steve Smith, Alan Morris, Michael Glass

TV-am is a new independent television company established under an IBA franchise to broadcast early morning 'breakfast' television programmes on a national basis across Britain. The spirit of this new television enterprise and the scope for developing a building which would be used as a visual backdrop for the media was from the outset considered integral to the brief.

The site in central London backs onto the Regent's Park Union Canal (an element in Nash's original scheme for Regent's Park) and faces onto Hawley Crescent and is surrounded by small-scale run-down commercial and industrial buildings. The area has recently begun to be revitalised by the presence of a thriving street market and an increasing number of small shops. The brief essentially was for new premises comprising two new television studios, associated technical and production areas and all office, administrative and conference facilities. With TV-am scheduled to go on air two years from the time of their being granted a franchise, a very fast track programme was required. The building was constructed with a design and build package to a construction budget of £4 million for 100,000 ft².

The new premises comprise part new building and part conversion of an existing 1930s industrial garage built on two floors with an existing large central void of irregular shape. The original garage building at the back of the site on the canal bank was retained whilst the various and more recent buildings that had been added along the street frontage were demolished to provide space for the studios and technical facilities and an access courtyard.

Extended captions throughout the illustrations for this building describe the composite nature of the design and the detailed nature of the completed exterior.

Inside, the main elements of the space, the hospitality suite, staircase and the converted existing bridge are unitied by an appropriate 'storyline' (east/west, sunrise/sunset, news from all over the world). The hospitality suite becomes a Japanese temple, the staircase a Messopotamian ziggurat, the bridge a classical temple, and the cul-de-sac at the other end a far western desert with Dallas mirrorglass facade.

Furniture and fittings were included in the commission, many being specially designed and purpose built. The building in use fulfills many first thoughts on its potential media image; egg cups are used as prizes fo viewers' quiz programmes, a computer draughted abstract of the 'keystone' introduces programmes, and the atrium is frequently used as a back drop to pop shows and interviews, and indeed has in effect, become a third studio.

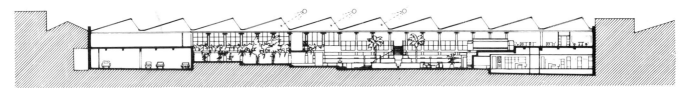

8 Long section through full length of atrium. Existing east light roof is retained; car parking is on the left at ground level, offices on the first floor and technical areas on right at ground floor

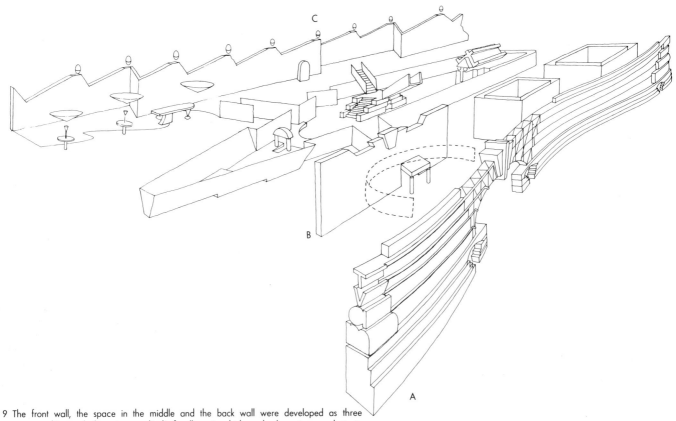

9 The front wall, the space in the middle and the back wall were developed as three separate architectural elements as a kind of collage in which each element responds to its context; the front wall to the undistinguished crescent-shaped street; the back wall to the canal; the interior to the existing retained building. The totality aimed for was that of a composite or village, and not that of a single corporate identity

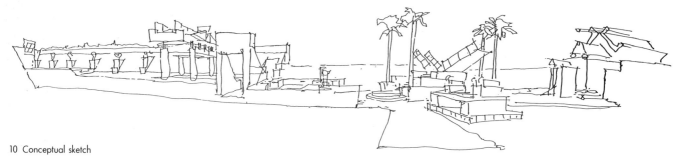

10 Conceptual sketch

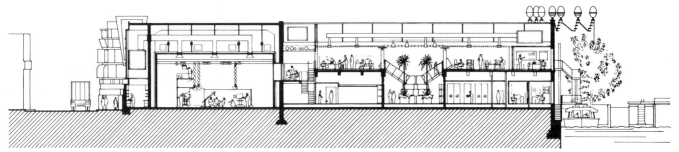

11 Cross (short) section. The new studio structures are on the left facing Hawley Crescent. The retained existing building on the right, offices are above technical areas looking into the atrium; on the extreme right is the Regents Canal

22 Interior of atrium — from a similar view point to that of the existing interior (below left)
23 Photo of inside before conversion
24 Photo of atrium in use for TV show

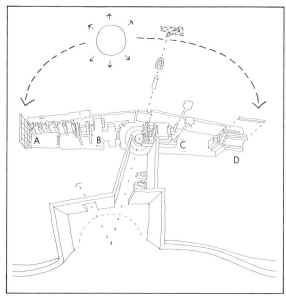

25 The global atrium garden, in four areas from east to west (A = Mid-West, B = Mediteranean, C = Mesopotamian, D = Oriental)

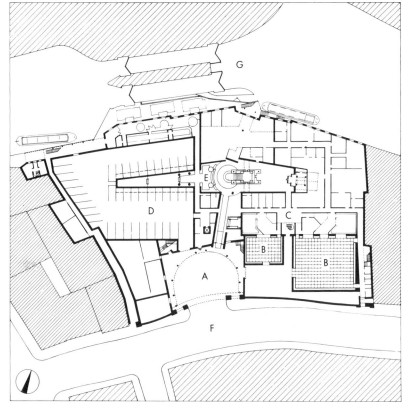

28 First floor plan

KEY

A Entrance courtyard
B The studios
C Technical areas
D Car parking
E Atrium gardens
F Hawley Crescent
G Regents Canal
H First floor offices
I Courtyard balcony

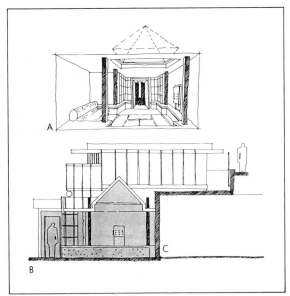

26 Sections through east end of atrium and the hospitality room within the eastern temple
27 Sections through west end of atrium: inclined walls to accommodate concealed car parking create narrow funnelled perspective effect terminating at Cactus Gardens & Dallas mirror glass wall

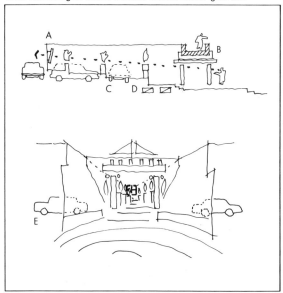

29 Ground floor plan

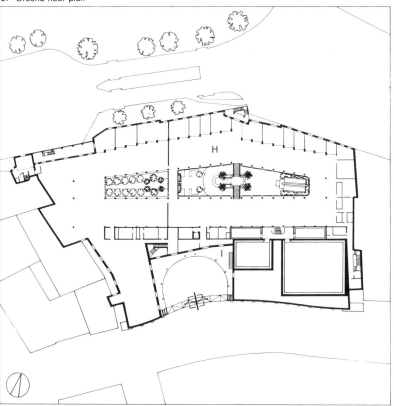

30 Canalside house with existing terraced housing (right) and local pleasure boat terminus in foreground
31 Western half of rear wall; new windows inserted, parapets raised and stepped and rough brickwork painted

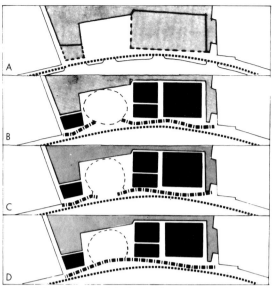

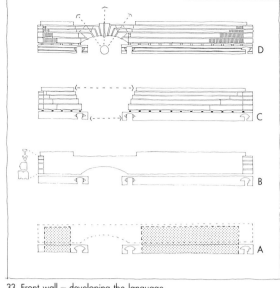

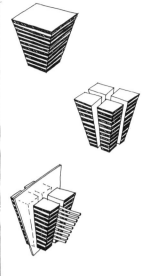

32 Establishing the curve of the front wall in response to the street

33 Front wall – developing the language

34 An abstracted 'keystone' identifies the entrance

35 North wall – zones (A = old brewery wall, B = TV-am mooring, C = sluice/chairman, and office, D = terace cafeteria, E = private mooring, F = the house)

36 North wall – transformation (A = existing stage, B = adding and modifying, C = silhouette, D = colour and language)

37 Elevation, detail and section of back wall

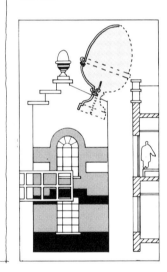

38 Inside the retained building the plinth is extended all around the existing central void at ground level

39 The rear wall before conversion (compare with 31)

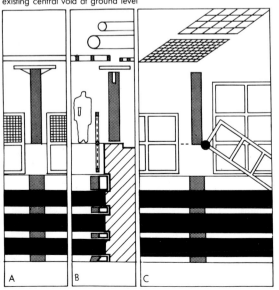

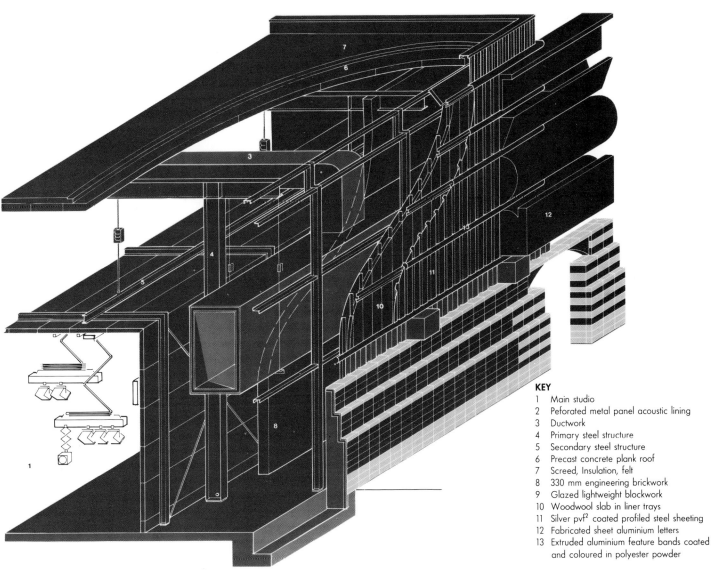

KEY

1 Main studio
2 Peforated metal panel acoustic lining
3 Ductwork
4 Primary steel structure
5 Secondary steel structure
6 Precast concrete plank roof
7 Screed, Insulation, felt
8 330 mm engineering brickwork
9 Glazed lightweight blockwork
10 Woodwool slab in liner trays
11 Silver pvf^2 coated profiled steel sheeting
12 Fabricated sheet aluminium letters
13 Extruded aluminium feature bands coated and coloured in polyester powder

40 The grey and black glazed block plinth is vandal proof, and above it the construction and colours are much lighter in colour and form — a vertical progression from dark/solid to light carried through all three elements. For acoustic reasons no windows were possible in the front wall which became an applied billboard fronting the studios immediately behind. Silver coloured industrial metal sheeting of different profiles, interspersed with the bands of colour suggesting sunrise, (and taken from the station's own logo) clad the walls

41,42 The ends of the front wall, given prominence by the curve of the street, are used to locate large scale logos

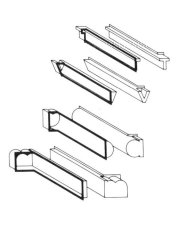

43 Resolving the off-centred entrance and arch to stage door

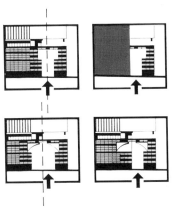

44 The connecting lattice arch is open to reduce wind resistance

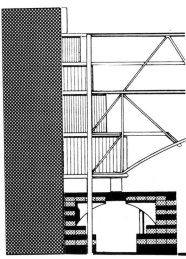

RADIO HEADQUARTERS 1982-83

Portland Place, London
for the British Broadcasting Corporation.

TF with John Chatwin, Mike Glass, Colin Leisk, Simon Sturgis, Gary Young*

In the summer of 1982, Terry Farrell Partnership were selected, from an international shortlist, as one of ten architectural practices to make a submission to the British Broadcasting Corporation, and the Terry Farrell Partnership presentation was one of three who were finally shortlisted to present to the full board.

1 Core building flanked by existing garden and Langham Pavilion

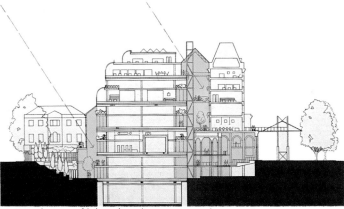

2 Core building flanked by new buildings

3 Vertical atriums of light and circulation routes are shown in yellow

4 Langham place entrance with new pavilion and atrium

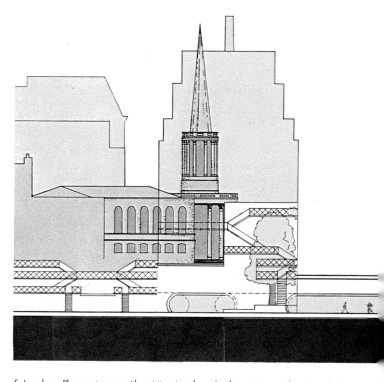

5 Langham Place entrance with existing Langham Pavilion atrium with restored Owen Jones entrance lobby and porte cochère/canopy

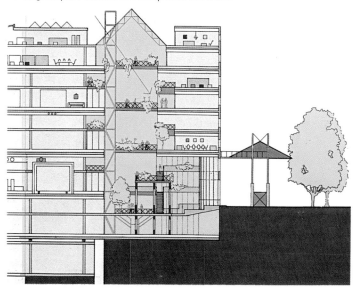

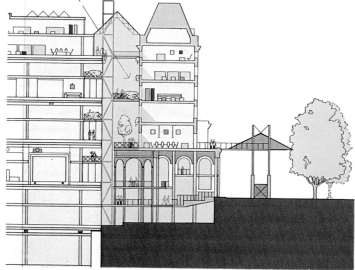

6 Existing Langham frontage

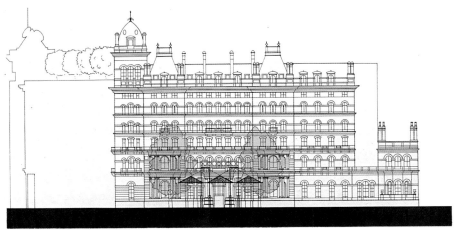

7 Restored frontage with reinstated roofline and porte cochère

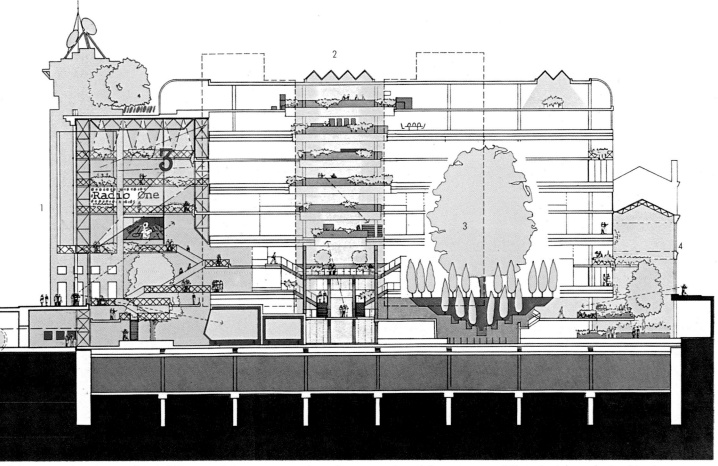

8 Long section through core: All Souls (left); BBC High Street connects under road to new complex with four major spaces: 1 Electronic window and atrium 2 Langham entrance 3 Retained garden on Cavendish Place 4 Conservatory atrium on Chandos Street

9 Owen Jones drawing from the V & A   10 Restored Owen Jones interiors with Langham Pavilion   11 New Pavilion: design studies   12 New Pavilion: long section through entrance atrium

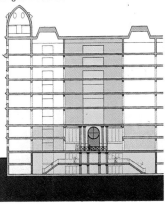

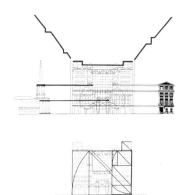

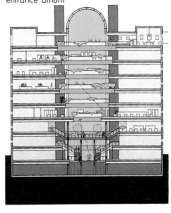

The BBC, perhaps more than any other single institution in this country, could be seen as the repository of popular cultural taste. It is appropriate, therefore, that this proposal is based on two strong concepts firmly rooted in popular appreciation of buildings and spaces. The first is that of the 'Gentle Giant': a major national institution gaining the strength from its size and resources to be responsive to context when undertaking major development, not requiring to display ostentatiously its technological might, capable of repairing environmental wounds, and preferring incremental and multi-layered solutions. The second concept is that of the 'City within the City': a sequence of spaces and buildings which, by their organisational structure and architectural relationships, are the more able to make their contribution to the larger city plan because of the strength of their own plan; the 'village high street' of the BBC set within the major Portland Place/Langham Place/Regent Street sequences designed by John Nash.

It was, however, envisaged that any new radio broadcasting facility would have to be capable of providing very considerable spatial flexibility, whilst at the same time achieving acoustic standards of the highest order. All this was to be achieved on a site, already in the ownership of the BBC, prominently terminating the view south down

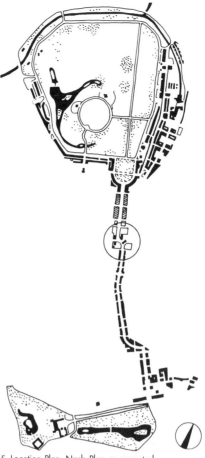
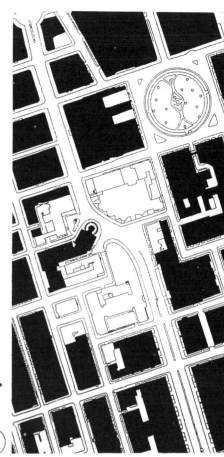

15 Location Plan: Nash Plan as executed

16 Site Plan: The 'BBC Village' including Langham Hotel site

13 The London 'village' of the Inns of Court (same scale as 16)

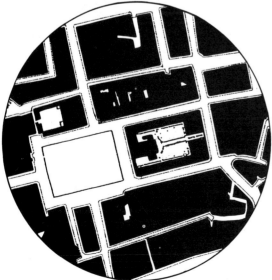

14 The London 'village' of Covent Garden

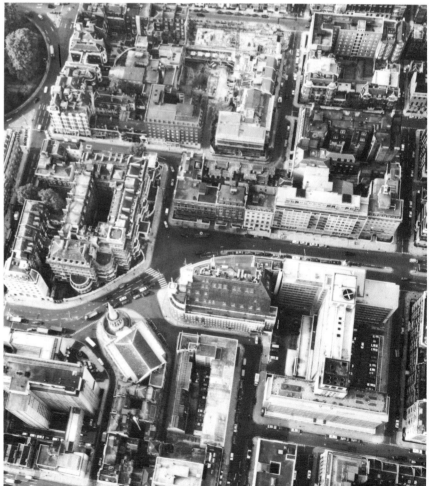

17 Aerial view of Portland Place

18 Existing buildings

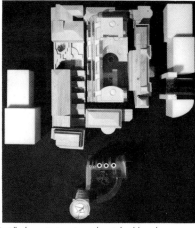

19 All elements to mix and match old and new

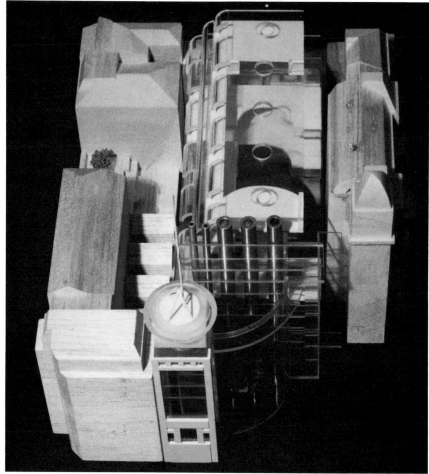

20 New core with existing perimeter buildings
21 New core with almost all new perimeter

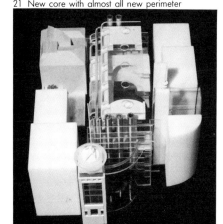

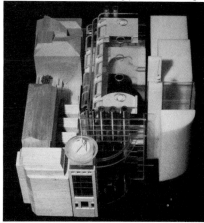

22 New core with 50% existing perimeter buildings

Portland Place from Regent's Park and at the central pivotal point of one of the finest sequences of urban spaces in London.

The main elements to emerge from initial technical studies were the identification of a 'core' of activities, people, spaces and equipment which formed the essential elements of radio broadcasting — as opposed to purely administrative or back-up facilities. Technical considerations tended to generate potential solutions more appropriate to 'open' green field sites. However, the site available — besides already being owned by the BBC — has an enormous advantage in its central London position.

It became clear that by carrying out limited demolition only at the centre of the site, (the light-well and rear bedroom wings of the Langham Hotel only) a core building could be constructed comprising ten structural bays. This central operation core or 'all-purpose-radio-space' as it was decided to call it provided the key to a more relaxed development of the perimeter of the site; by allowing the retention of the main range of the Langham Hotel, and frontage properties in Cavendish Place and Chandos Street, the design and construction programme for the core (the 'Gentle Giant') could proceed with absolute certainty while discussion and consideration of the Langham frontage and other listed buildings on the site continued ensuring that the right perimeter contextual solution would in time emerge. The retention and incorporation of these buildings within the scheme to provide the back-up and ancillary spaces was quite feasible; in the longer term their incremental redevelopment as extensions to the central core would provide considerable flexibility at a low cost.

23 Conceptual sketch

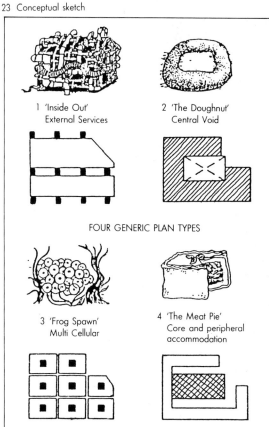

1 'Inside Out' External Services

2 'The Doughnut' Central Void

FOUR GENERIC PLAN TYPES

3 'Frog Spawn' Multi Cellular

4 'The Meat Pie' Core and peripheral accommodation

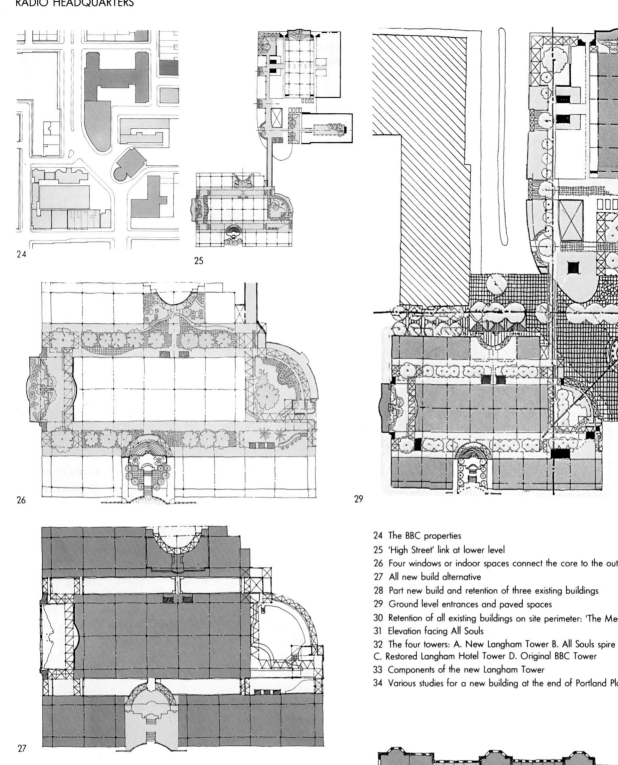

24

25

26

29

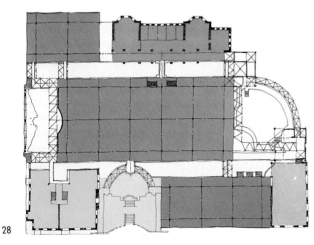

27

28

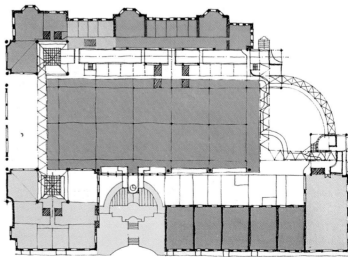

30

24 The BBC properties
25 'High Street' link at lower level
26 Four windows or indoor spaces connect the core to the outside world
27 All new build alternative
28 Part new build and retention of three existing buildings
29 Ground level entrances and paved spaces
30 Retention of all existing buildings on site perimeter: 'The Meat Pie'
31 Elevation facing All Souls
32 The four towers: A. New Langham Tower B. All Souls spire
C. Restored Langham Hotel Tower D. Original BBC Tower
33 Components of the new Langham Tower
34 Various studies for a new building at the end of Portland Place

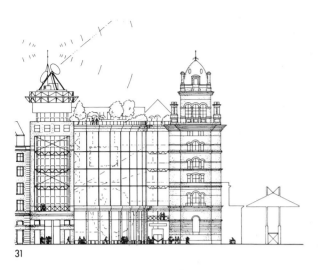

31

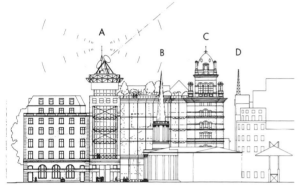

A   B   C   D

32

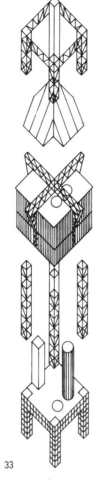

33

A MEAT PIE POEM

*A Master Cook! Why
He's the Man of Men,
He paints, he carves
He builds, he fortifies
Makes Citadels of
Curious fowl and fish.
Some he dry ditches,
Some moats around
With broths, mounts
Marrow bones, cuts
Fifty angled customs,
Rears bulwark pies,
And for his outer
Works, raiseth rampards
Of immortal crust!*

Ben Jonson, early 17thC

34

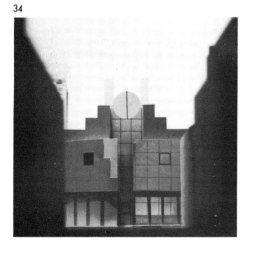

TELEVISION STUDIOS
1982-83
West India Docks, London
for Limehouse Productions

TF with Laurence Bain, John Chatwin, Michael Glass, Steve Ibbotson, Peter Jenkins, John Langley, John Letherland, Satish Patel, Jeremy Peacock, Oliver Richards*, Simon Sturgis, Clive Wilkinson

2 Six add-on elements, seen from Limehouse's boat

3 The narrow quayside restricts view points to oblique angles (see also 1 opposite)

4 Entrance frame with projecting lobby

5 Frame enclosing star dressing rooms on mezzanine floor

These studios were built for Limehouse Productions, a company founded to be an independent technical and creative centre for the production of programmes, both for established television markets and the fast-growing independent sector.

These new premises comprise conversions and extensions to a 1952-built rum and banana warehouse on Canary Wharf, in the heart of London's docklands. The siting of the new production centre, in an area that for a long time has suffered from the decline of London as a major shipping port, was greatly encouraged by the financial incentives offered in this area as an Enterprise Zone. The existing warehouse was a large three-storey brick and concrete frame building of rugged simplicity.

The brief called for the creation of two television studios designed to very high technical specifications for lighting and sound, with all attendant production, office and workshop facilities. A requirement was also for a very short design and construction period and a fast track management contract was adopted.

Internally the major changes were for the construction of the two studios. These were created by demolishing part of the existing concrete floors, walls and ceilings. A new mezzanine floor was added along the north entrance frontage to provide additional 'area for performers' dressing rooms and related facilities. At ground level a large reception area acts as the main focus of the building, leading to the main stair and lift, the studios and production areas, and the public client rooms.

Externally, six major elements were added to the north elevation to provide additional accommodation and be the obvious new built elements on the entry side which would then give the building an identity. These are large in size and closely related in appearance and of a scale which links the new additions and the massive bulk of the existing warehouse. They are constructed of vitreous enamelled steel panels in four colours and with plinths of glazed ceramic blocks. A 45° angle geometry is used to integrate the new internal spaces formed by these add-ons to existing spaces and to give external expression to key 'ceremonial' elements such as the star dressing rooms, client suites, the production managers' office and the main entrance. Six large abstracted bird shapes symbolise the building's waterside location and the spirit of communication.

A large plant room, required by the complex servicing requirements, is situated at roof level. The south and east elevations remain essentially as found, with the additions of an escape stair, an electricity sub-station, and louvres or solid infill panels where required by internal constraints. Specially designed seating and a reception desk in the main entrance are constructed of laminate, cotton fabric and black and white marble.

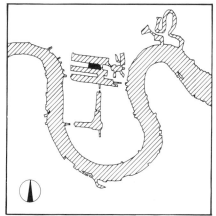

6 Location Plan: Isle of Dogs

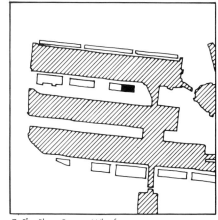

7 Site Plan: Canary Wharf

8 Existing building inside
9 Existing building, north (entrance) facade

10 North facade, after conversion, viewed from Billingsgate Fish Market

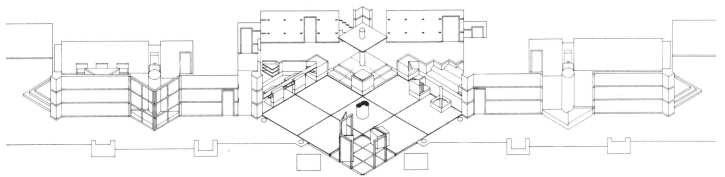

11 Plan of linear circulation routes which project out from existing building at ground level

12 Detail of centre part of ground level plan, showing 45° rotated entrance hall with reception, seating and draught lobby

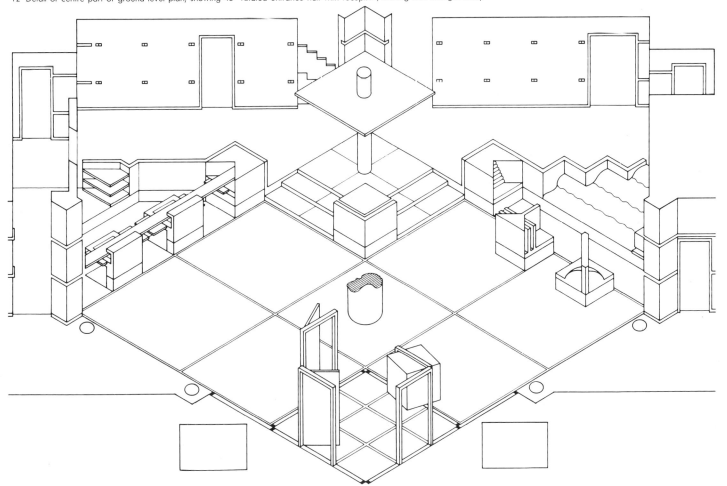

13

14  15

13 Entrance hall viewed from behind the reception desk

14 Entrance hall: 'Maypole' column and draught lobby

15 Detail: rear steps with studio entrances beyond

16

17

18

16 Entrance hall viewed from the seating in waiting area

17 Ground level access corridor looking towards entrance hall with similar corridor in distance

18 Detail: entrance hall seats

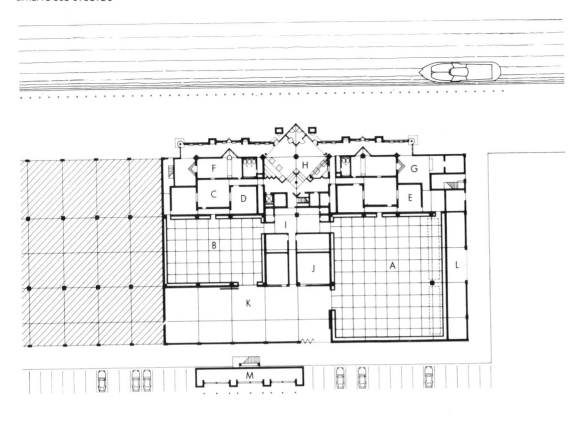

KEY

A Studio 1 (6000 sq ft)
B Studio 2 (3000 sq ft)
C Production Control
D Sound Control
E Lighting Control
F Client Room
G Audience Lobby
H Reception
I Artist's Assembly
J Technical Stores
K Scenery
L Technical Workshop
M L.E.B.

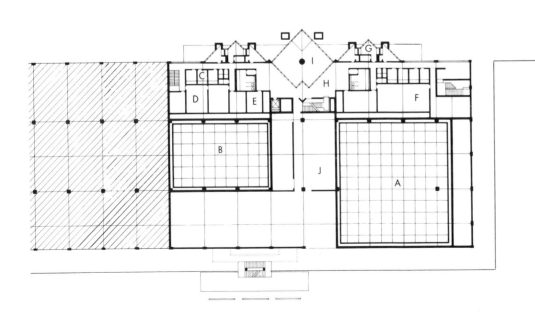

20 Mezzanine level plan:

KEY

A Studio 1
B Studio 2
C Dressing rooms
D Crowd dressing
E Make-up
F Wardrobe
G Star dressing rooms
H Green room
I Void to reception
J Expansion space

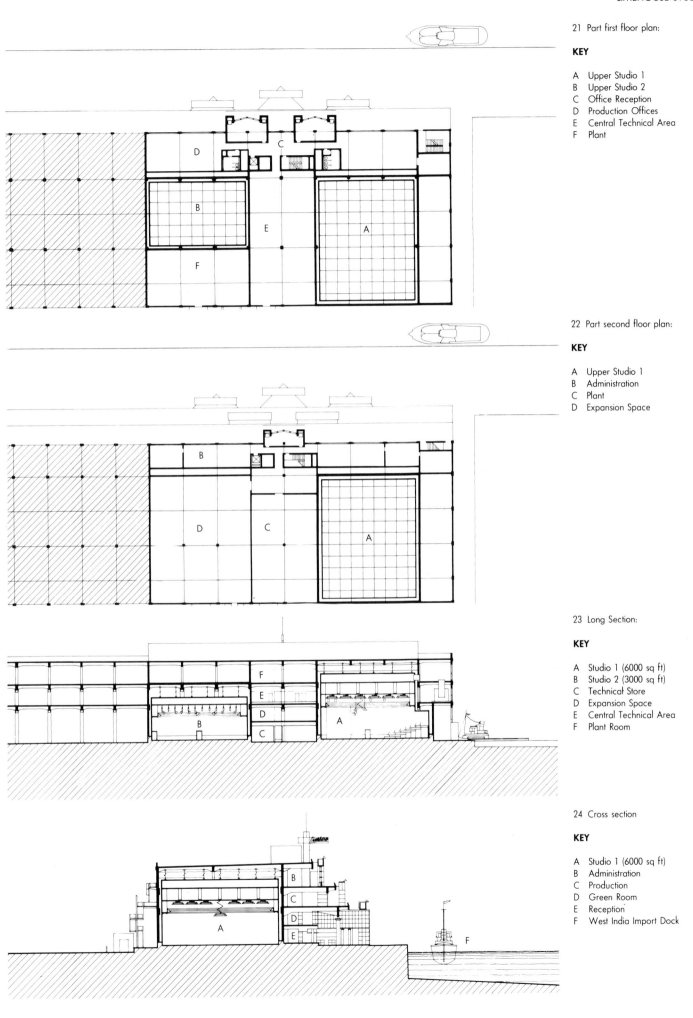

21 Part first floor plan:

KEY

A Upper Studio 1
B Upper Studio 2
C Office Reception
D Production Offices
E Central Technical Area
F Plant

22 Part second floor plan:

KEY

A Upper Studio 1
B Administration
C Plant
D Expansion Space

23 Long Section:

KEY

A Studio 1 (6000 sq ft)
B Studio 2 (3000 sq ft)
C Technical Store
D Expansion Space
E Central Technical Area
F Plant Room

24 Cross section

KEY

A Studio 1 (6000 sq ft)
B Administration
C Production
D Green Room
E Reception
F West India Import Dock

25 Entrance steps to client's suite

26 Typical upper corridor

27 Interior of client's suite

28a,b Details of interior of client's suite

28a

28b

29 Rear elevation with new electrical transformer building and escape stairs

30 Control room to main studio

31 Interior of main studio

THE TRIANGLES, MANSION HOUSE

Alternative Proposals for Rehabilitation of Existing Buildings 1983-84 London

TF with Sumaya Bardawil, John Chatwin, Joe Foges, John Langley*, Laurie Pocza

This scheme was prepared for the conservation group 'Save Britain's Heritage' as an alternative to the scheme to build a 25-storey tower block and attendant formal plaza designed by Mies van der Rohe, and proposed by a private developer for the site. The basis of the scheme was for the retention of a fine and unique collection of Victorian buildings threatened by demolition under the Mies proposals.

The site is at the heart of the historic centre of the City of London and the scheme is concerned with four triangular blocks of buildings that create an intricate series of intersections and several major architectural corner set pieces. Most of the buildings were developed between 1870 and 1900 and the richness and variety in particular is unique within the City.

The aims of the scheme are to preserve and enrich the experience of City life at street level in this area and to give the existing buildings of character a useful long-term extension to their life. Existing narrow streets are pedestrianised, new pedestrian arcades are formed to provide sheltered new access to office buildings and the London underground, and canopies are provided over shopfronts. These changes, together with the narrowing of Queen Victoria Street to three lanes with a pedestrian centre island, all improve the existing qualities of pedestrian movement and retain the character of the streets and narrow walkways of the City.

Public spaces in the City tend to be for the most part small in scale, often intricate, enclosed and invariably informal. Two new small spaces are proposed, a courtyard and a semi-private courtyard/office precinct — Triangle Chambers. Existing spaces are reinforced by semi-enclosure, landscaping and street closure to provide for sheltered seating in areas that catch the midday sun.

Shopping is retained and rationalised at ground floor level. New shopping is added at basement level. The existing upper office floors are re-serviced and rationalised to provide eleven new office chambers ranging from 4 to 12,000 square feet, each with their own off-street front door.

Given the quality of the existing buildings, external architectural alterations are restricted to re-designing the existing inferior shopfronts and to the addition of further service areas and office accommodation at roof level in a manner that adds to the already vigorous skyline.

1 Three old City of London site plans a) Portion of Braun and Hogenberg's Plan 1572 b) Portion of Faithorne and Newcourt's Plan 1650 c) Portion of Pine and Tinney's Plan 1742

2 Three contemporary engravings from *The Builder*

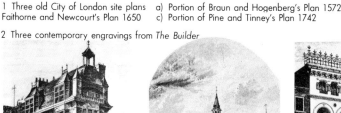

a) Nos 4 & 5 Poultry   b) Mappin & Webb   c) No 1 Poultry

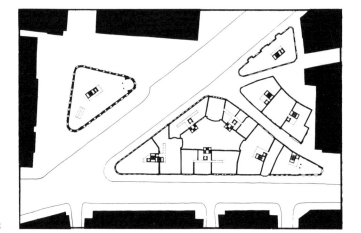

3

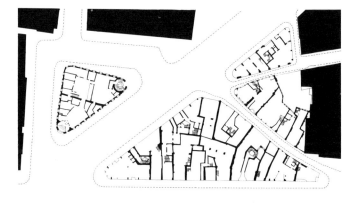

4

3 Typical existing upper floor plan

4 Existing ground floor plan

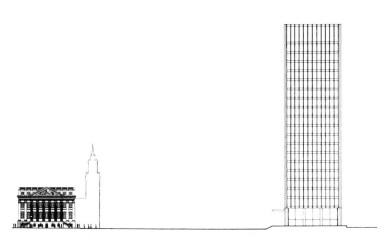

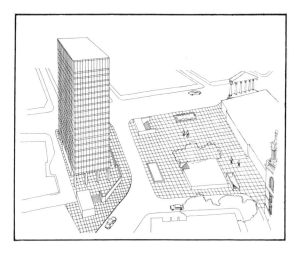

5,6 Suggested elevation and aerial view of the Mies Tower and Piazza (TFP)

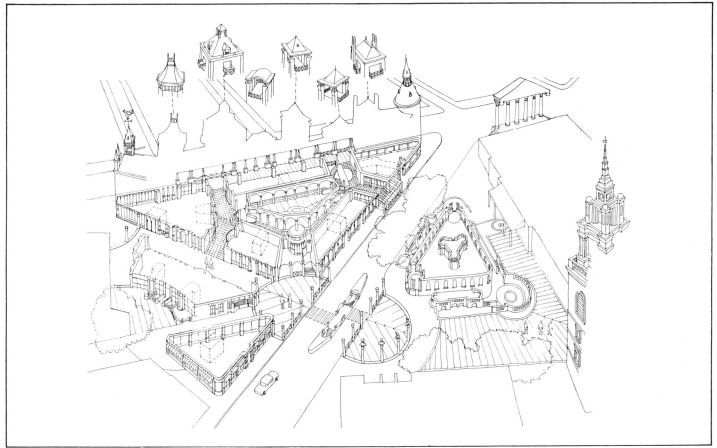

7 The primary interventions are at ground level and roof level with the facades between restored

8 Part elevation of Poultry facades as restored and added to

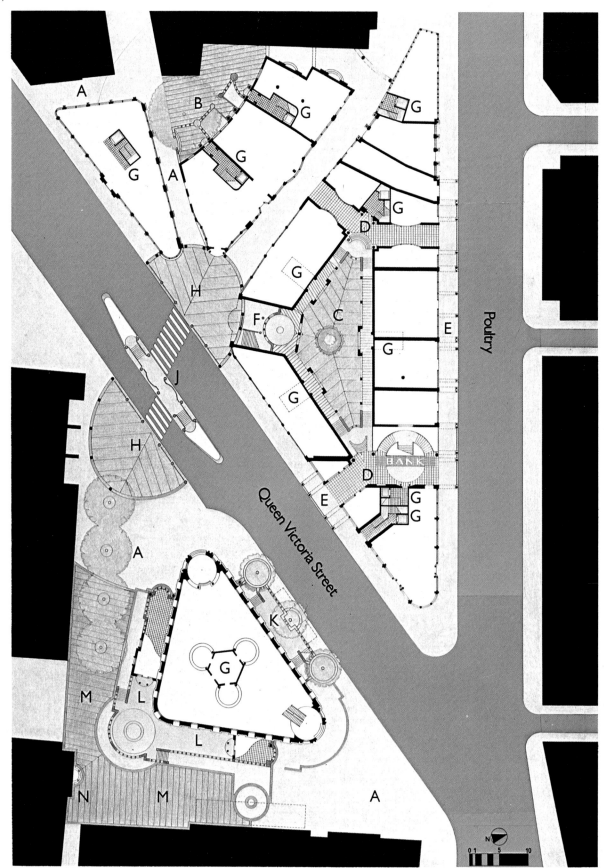

9 Proposed Ground Level Plan

KEY

A Five Streets pedestrianised
B New courtyard – gives access to refurbished office chambers above and "spillover" space to extended wine bars and pubs
C Triangle Chambers – new upper level courtyard with perimeter arcade
D New public arcades – providing access to Triangle

Chambers, arcade shops and an eastern arcade to Tube station
E New canopies to provide weather protected pavement
F Additional Tube access via lower shopping area
G Eleven refurbished office elements grouped more efficiently around individual lift, stair and service cores "Spillover" sitting space for adjacent restaurants, pubs and wine bars

H Reduction of Queen Victoria Street by one lane (southbound) to provide landscaped area in front of
J New Zealand Bank Buildings and central island
K Landscaping around lower area with Roman antiquities display and new access to Tube
L Lower coffee bars and terraces
M "Spillover" sitting space and landscaped precinct
N Monument/screen to hide addition to St Stephen, Walbrook

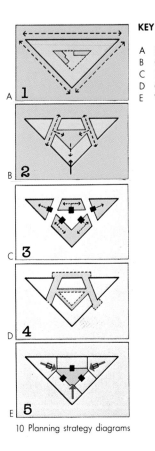

KEY

A Existing block
B Ground level routes
C New office cores
D Covered routes
E Views into courtyard

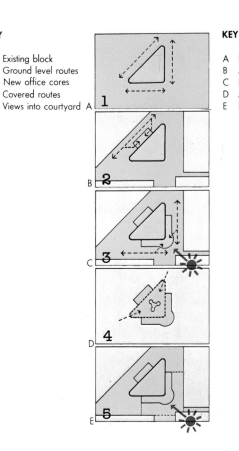

KEY

A Existing block
B Access to Underground
C Lower level coffee shop
D Access to building above
E New public courtyard

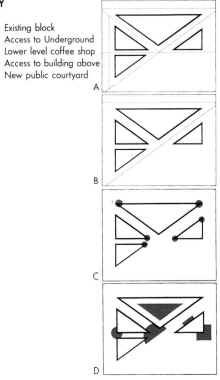
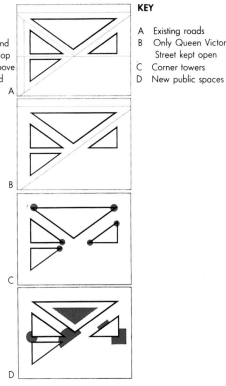

KEY

A Existing roads
B Only Queen Victoria
    Street kept open
C Corner towers
D New public spaces

10 Planning strategy diagrams

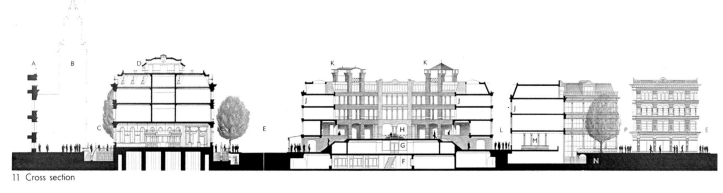

11 Cross section

KEY

A Mansion House by Dance
B St Stephen, Walbrook, by Wren
C New lower terraces, coffee bar and tube access
D Refurbished Bank of New Zealand with restored attic floor and new rooftop boardroom and plant area
E Queen Victoria Street
F Lower concourse — access to tubes with some shopping
G New central shop or wine bar
H New Upper office precinct, Triangle Chambers
I Refurbished offices above ground floor
J shopping
K New stair and lift towers servicing refurbished offices with boardrooms and plant at the top
L levels
M Bucklersbury
N Existing pubs and wine bars extended
O Rear landscaped courtyard
P St Pancras Lane
Q Mappin & Webb and Mansion House Chambers with restored shopfront
R Main canopies to through arcades
S Minor canopies to central shops
T Rebuilt no 2 Poultry: extends no 1 and provides lift, stair and service core to 1, 2 and 3 Poultry
U Blank gable and party walls opened up to provide windows and balconies on all flanks
V New rooftop boardroom suites and plant rooms

12 Elevation from Mansion House and along Poultry

MIXED DEVELOPMENT OF AN HISTORIC TRIANGULAR ISLAND SITE

Covent Garden, London

TF with John Chatwin, Gary Young, Jim Corcoran, Steve Ibbotson*, Jonathan McDowell, Simon Sturgis* Completion in phases 1984/5.

Thirty seventeenth- and eighteenth-century buildings have been in the clients' ownership for 250 years and are being restored around a new central paved courtyard with two new infill corner buildings. The scheme incorporates a wide range of shops, housing units, offices and includes a restoration of the clients' own ironmongery shop and showroom.

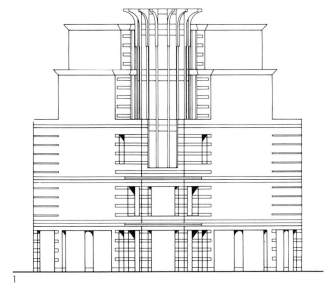

1

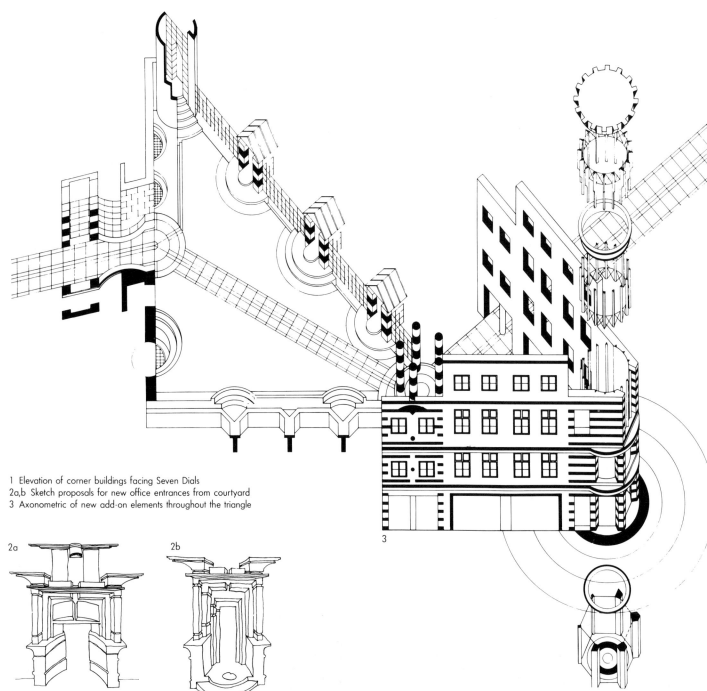

1 Elevation of corner buildings facing Seven Dials
2a,b Sketch proposals for new office entrances from courtyard
3 Axonometric of new add-on elements throughout the triangle

2a

2b

3

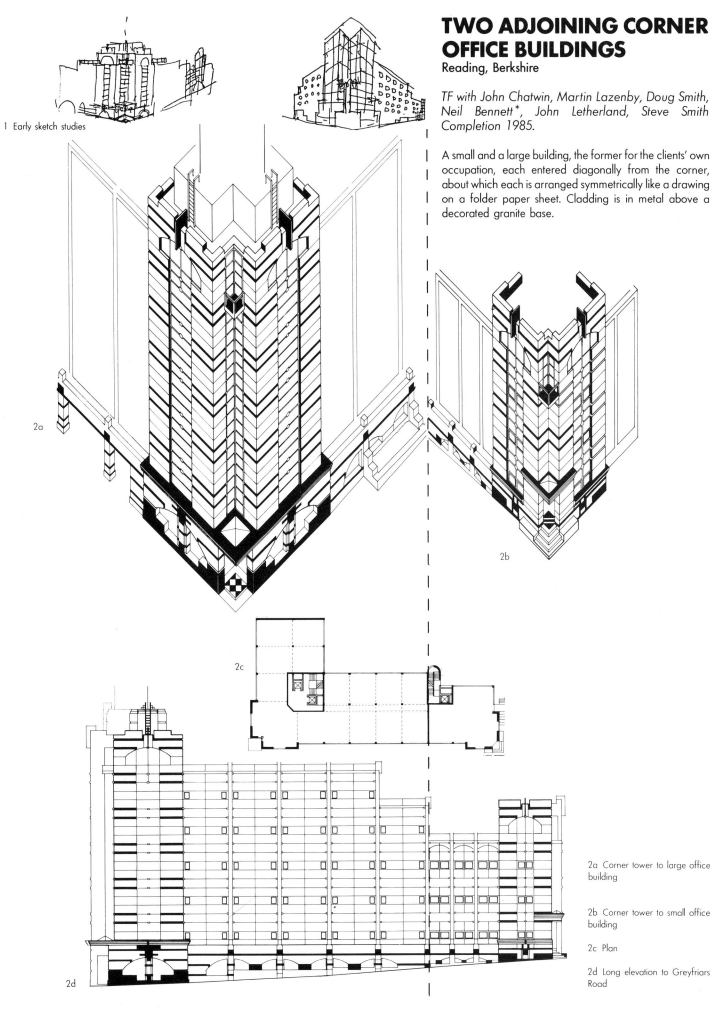

TWO ADJOINING CORNER OFFICE BUILDINGS
Reading, Berkshire

TF with John Chatwin, Martin Lazenby, Doug Smith, Neil Bennett*, John Letherland, Steve Smith Completion 1985.

A small and a large building, the former for the clients' own occupation, each entered diagonally from the corner, about which each is arranged symmetrically like a drawing on a folder paper sheet. Cladding is in metal above a decorated granite base.

1 Early sketch studies

2a

2b

2c

2d

2a Corner tower to large office building

2b Corner tower to small office building

2c Plan

2d Long elevation to Greyfriars Road

BANKING BUILDING
Queen Street, City of London

TF with Andrew Cowan*, John Chatwin, Michael Donovan, Doug Streeter, Thierry Reinhardt, Andrew Hobson
Completion 1985.

Located on the edge of a conservation area with one major street frontage the building is conceived as dual pavilions each the scale of the surrounding older buildings, linked by entrance portico and rooftop double volume boardroom. Cladding is in a variety of granites of differing colours and finishing textures.

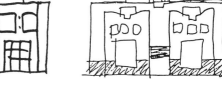

1 Early sketch studies

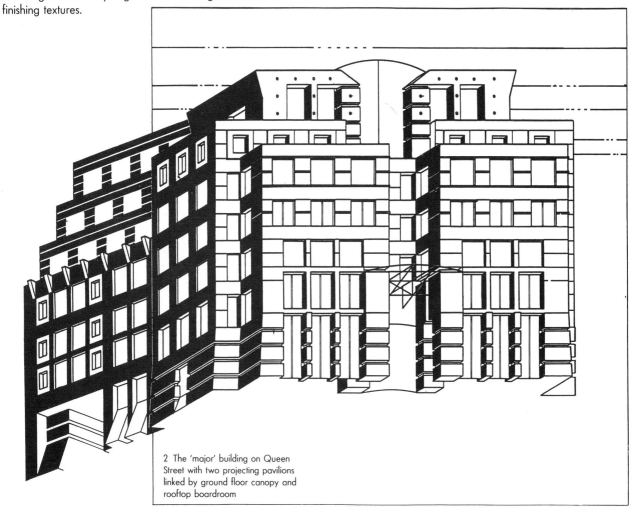

2 The 'major' building on Queen Street with two projecting pavilions linked by ground floor canopy and rooftop boardroom

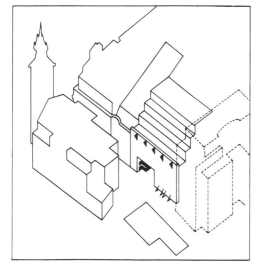

3 Skinner's Lane 'minor' building

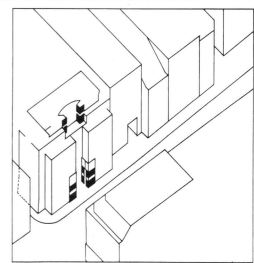

4 Queen Street 'major' building

1 Early sketch studies

OFFICES AND BANKS
1983-86
Aldgate Pump Site, City of London

TF with John Chatwin, Gary Young, Clive Wilkinson *
Completion 1986.

The building, visible for some distance along the Aldgate entrance approach to the City incorporates the old Aldgate Pump memorial within the banking hall's entry rotunda. Other elements which reflect the building's unique corner site role in the urban scene are the office portico, cornice, string courses and corner column with boardroom 'capital'.

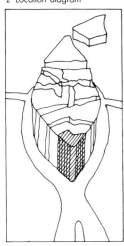

2 Location diagram

3 Corner column

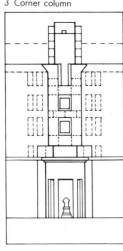

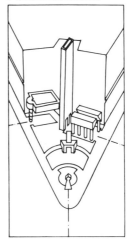

4 Ground level elements

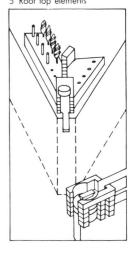

5 Roof top elements

CLUBHOUSE, HEADQUARTERS AND BOAT STORE

Henley, Berkshire
for Henley Royal Regatta

TF with Joe Foges, Doug Streeter
Completion 1985.*

The site is in a fine, semi-rural setting on the banks of the Thames facing the town of Henley and immediately adjacent to an eighteenth-century road bridge. Symmetrically planned at right angles to the river in the Thames timber boathouse tradition, the three-storey building has a different use on each level—the club secretary's dwelling at roof top, the clubhouse and administration facilities at middle (road) level and the boathouse at river level.

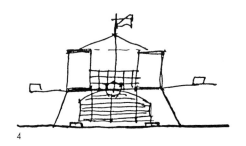

4

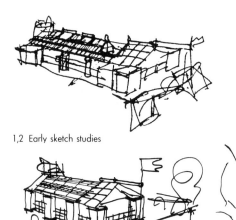

1,2 Early sketch studies

3 Photograph of existing buildings on site from across river

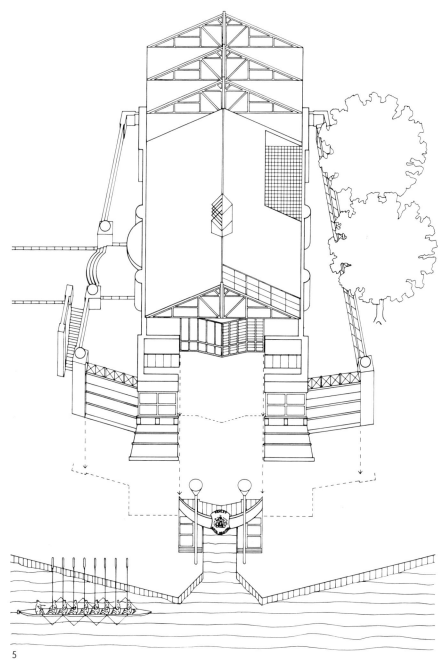

5

5 Axonometric
4,6,7 Early sketch studies

6　　　　　　　　7

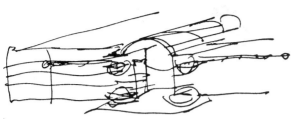

1 Early sketch study

FACTORY AND OFFICES
London
for Exhibition and Architectural lettering manufacturers

TF with John Chatwin and Craig Downie*
Completion 1984.

The company's own logo 'G' (for Graphex Ltd) was used to elaborate a simple neat functional box; the building's entrance is through a giant letter 'G' in colour finished aluminium framework. The top curve of the 'G' is extended right through the building, continuing the external identity in the form of a central rooflight which illuminates the first floor offices and workshop behind.

2 Axonometric

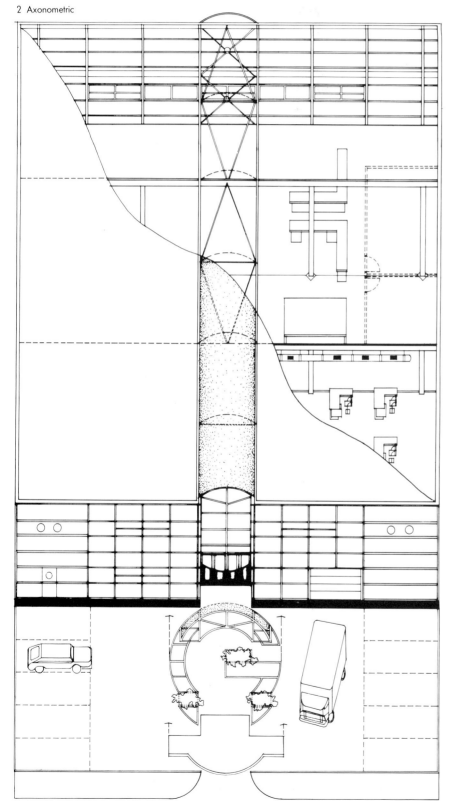

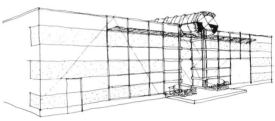

3,4 Early entrance studies

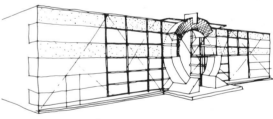

5 Entrance prior to completion

HAMMERSMITH BROADWAY

Island Site Development Proposals
Hammersmith, London 1984

TF with Sumaya Bardawil, John Chatwin, Laurie Pocza, David Quigley*, Doug Streeter

This development proposal was prepared as part of a report commissioned by the Greater London Council for a new town centre and transport interchange at Hammersmith in west London.

The brief for the proposals was prepared in conjunction with officers of the GLC and in intensive consultation with a number of local bodies and community groups. It developed as a requirement to prepare an overall scheme for the island site which would improve the environment, produce wider benefits in terms of public/community use and open space, and form a worthy centre for Hammersmith well integrated into its surroundings and the adjoining main shopping area. The proposals were to retain existing buildings where possible, avoid the need for major new land acquisition and be capable of rapid implementation as an improved transport interchange.

This interchange involves the building of a new bus station on the most immediately available and least valuable land, and the re-organisation and improvement of the existing northern underground concourse and southern ticket office.

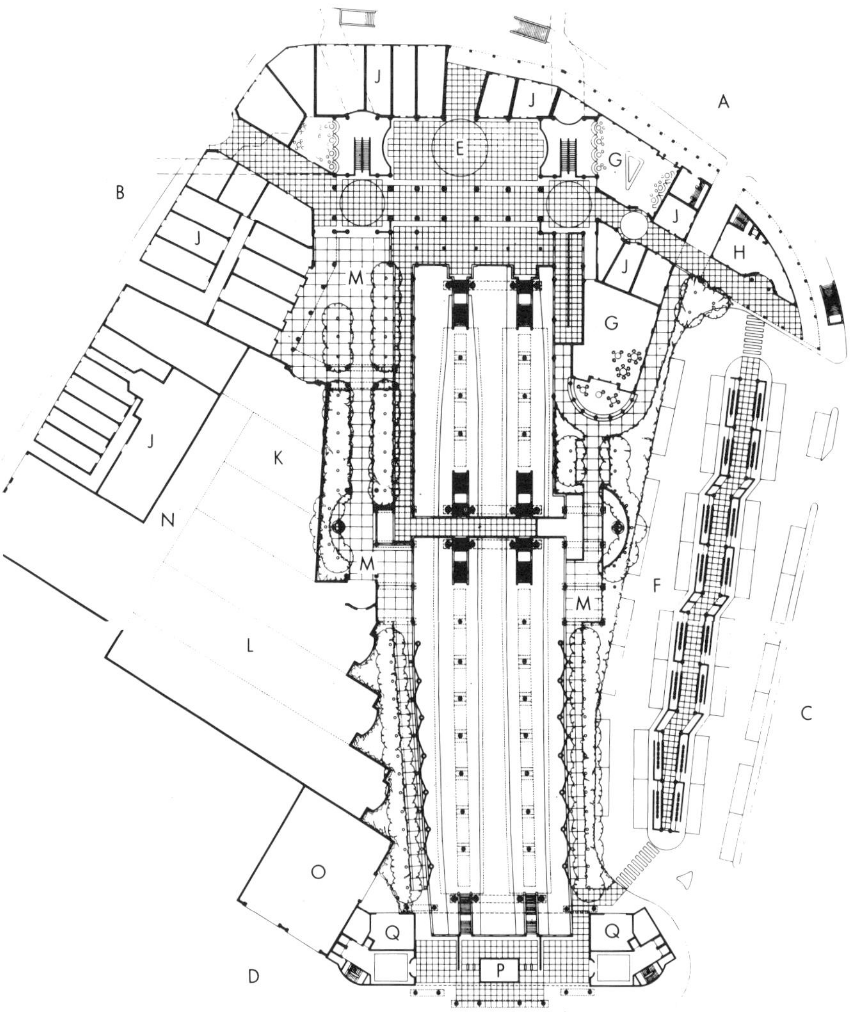

1 Plan of new proposals at concourse level

KEY

A   Broadway
B   Queen Caroline Street (as existing)
C   Butterwick
D   Talgarth Road
E   The underground station concourse
F   The new bus station
G   The restored Clarendon with ground level bus/underground link
H   London Transport Building
J   Shops, kiosks and other related uses
K   Possible major shop/store
L   Leisure centre
M   Pedestrian paths and gardens
N   Bradbury House restored
O   Bradbury House restored for leisure use
P   New southern ticket office
Q   Access to new building over south-east corner

2 Cross section

KEY

A   New underground concourse
B   New building over southern ticket office
C   Void over lower pedestrian concourse
D   Pedestrian link to bus station
E   Existing Clarendon assembly rooms restored
F   New Hammersmith Broadway bus station
G   Cellar Wine Bar and shopping
H   Pedestrian link to Metropolitan and North Broadway
I   Pedestrian link to bus station and East Hammersmith

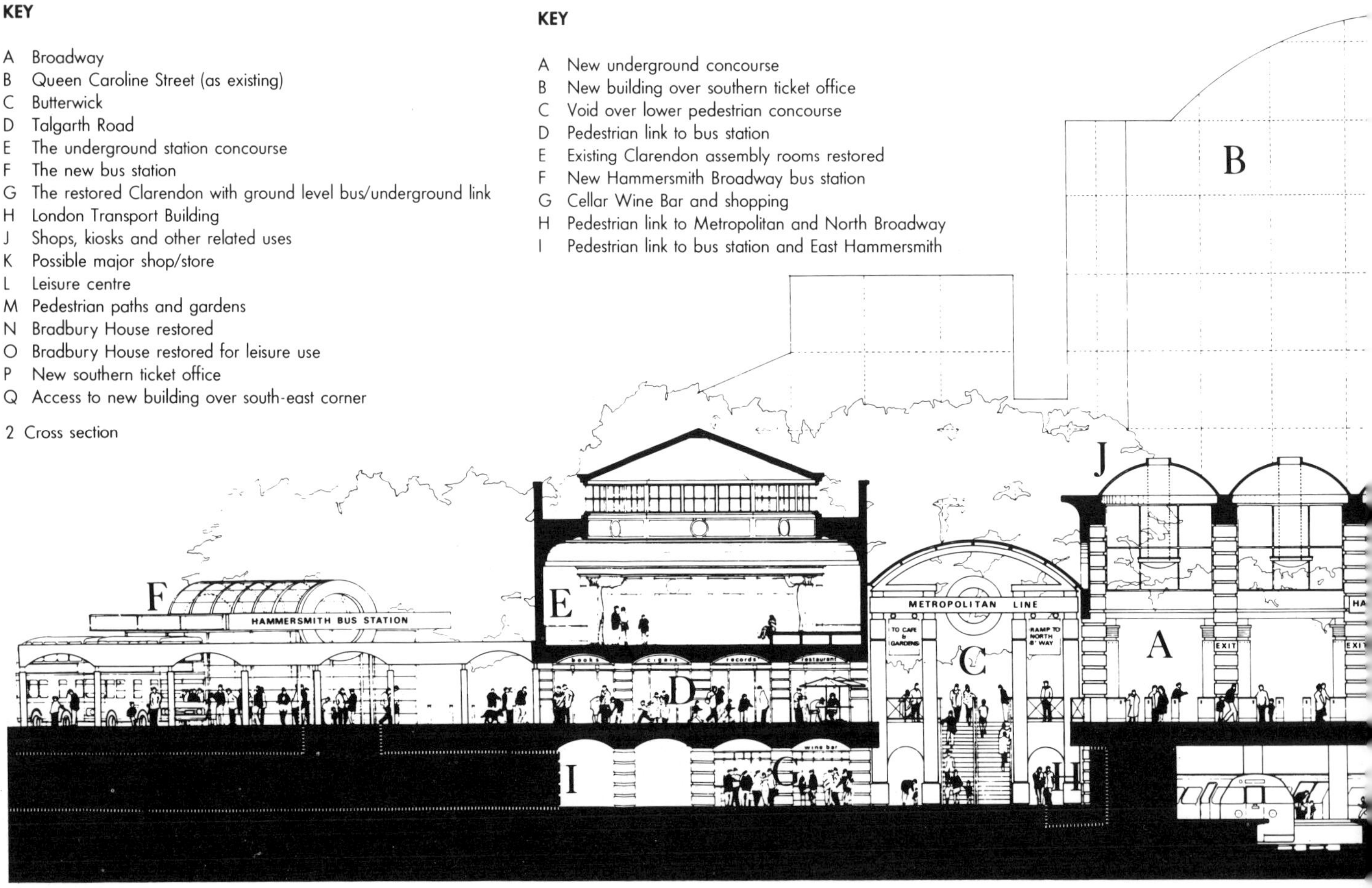

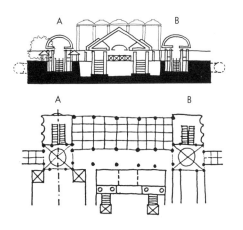

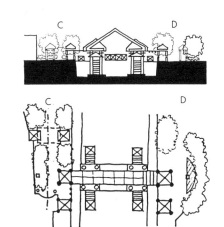

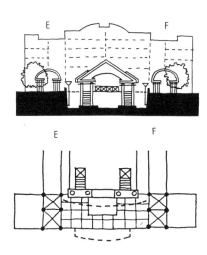

3, 4, 5 Three main architectural elements are proposed for the new public pathways and gardens planned within the centre of the island site. These are bridges, gateways and beacons. Bridges provide cover and visual focus to spaces and crossings based on the existing railway structures.

Gateways identify the major entrances and crossings along the routes of pedestrian movements and beacons provide for the orientation, direction finding and safety essential for successful urban pedestrian movement.

6 View of model

The urban regeneration involves retaining the bulk of existing buildings on the north and west of the site, thus releasing a large resource for immediate comprehensive revitalisation. Three existing buildings of note are to be restored. The formation of new covered arcades under the existing buildings along Hammersmith road allows for the development of the site irrespective of the already proposed road widening. New buildings are to be located on the edges of the site, giving the least demolition of existing buildings and maximum environmental protection to the town centre from roads to the south. The more protected internal environments thus created focus around two major public spaces axially arranged to focus on Broadway.

Such a strategy provides for an initial phase that can immediately be implemented and for the widest range of future options which can all be carried out in incremental stages, as opposed to a strategy of single comprehensive redevelopment. This characteristic and the fact that all public space and pedestrian movement is at ground level sharply contrasts this proposal with all previous ones.

J   New roof over part of concourse
K   Void over lower pedestrian concourse
L   Lower pedestrian link to King Street
M   Lower concourse shopping area
N   Pedestrian link to King Street and New Market Square
O   Upper part of shops and professional offices
P   Residential accommodation
Q   Existing Broadway buildings rehabilitated
R   Lower pedestrian link to St Paul's and West Hammersmith
S   New Market Square (later phase)
T   Existing underground platforms to be improved and upgraded

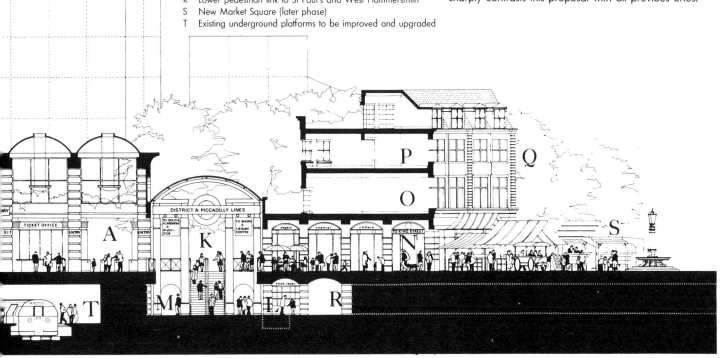

PRAGMATIC ART AND SPATIAL VIRTUOSITY

Colin Amery

As we approach the last decade of the twentieth century architects and their clients are caught in the cross-currents of aesthetic and political uncertainty. In Britain the architectural climate is as variable as the English weather. Since the Second World War some of the greatest strengths of the architectural profession have not been manifested in the productions of individual geniuses but in the development of public, socially concerned offices that have built largely for the denizens of the Welfare State. But there has been a parallel development of practices that have been able to work for universities or rich private business clients and develop a less uniform version of modern architecture. It is fair to say that architecture in Britain in the last fifty years has reflected all the currents of world thinking about architecture but it has usually done so somewhat after the event. In the same way as Palladianism came late to these shores, International Modernism arrived late, had its growth stunted by the war and flowered in the end rather pathetically. Afterward British architects like Terry Farrell, who were born as the Second World War began, educated by the State and able to start building in the economically booming 1960s, represent a very particular breed. It is a breed that has not been thoroughly examined.

It is important to look at origins and environment when considering the work of any architect and in Farrell's case, as a representative of the new kind of grammar school success, it is timely. The education provided by the grammar schools, before they were consumed by the vastness and mediocrity of the comprehensive system, was not elitist or dangerous, it was simply a continuation of the belief in academic learning and a certain ethos of character development based on competition. Those of us who were very aware in the 1950s and interested in the way of the world, were more than likely to have been subjected to one of two kinds of education. One route was the traditional English one loosely based on a classical source, and the other route was inspired by the American vision of the post-war highly technological world. Farrell's training as an architect, having survived the rigours of grammar school in Newcastle, encompassed both

these strands. Five years at the University of Durham probably heightened the desire to visit the New World which he accomplished by winning a Harkness Fellowship to follow up graduate studies in architecture and city planning at the University of Pennsylvania. It is hard today, when transatlantic commuting, especially for architects and their critic groupies is commonplace, to imagine the excitement of America in the early 1960s. America was, at least to a war-torn Europe about to try socialism, *the* place of the future. America in the 1960s appeared to offer so much to the free world. In architecture it had acted as a haven for the refugees from the Bauhaus and invented the idea of International Modern. In the capitalist world Mies van der Rohe, Walter Gropius, Chermayeff *et al* were seen as the creators of a new style. It was a style that suited capitalism as well as it suited socialism — because it was repetitive, easily commercialised and sufficiently abstract to be regarded as close to art. In America in the 1960s only the early hints of dissatisfaction with the all-powerful Modern Movement were beginning to be heard. It was to take the writings and lectures of Colin Rowe and the architecture and theory of Louis Khan and Robert Venturi to change the emphasis on super technology and to make architects aware of things like 'context', materials, symbolism and the meaning of architecture.

It is significant that Terry Farrell chose to work in America in a planning office (in Camden, New Jersey) rather than swing off into one of the major Modern Movement offices. It is the study of the town that has borne most fruit in some of the architects that are producing interesting buildings today. Colin Rowe introduced to a whole generation the idea of attempting to achieve a correspondence between architecture and urbanism. He made architects see, as their forebears had seen as a matter of course, that the city is the seed-bed of architectural culture. Modern Movement dogma had made the city the centre of a dualism, the management of people and buildings masqueraded as design and sometimes as art, when in fact it was simply political management. Farrell saw in America what Betjeman had warned us so clearly about:

> I have a vision of the future, chum,
> The worker's flats in fields of soya beans,
> Towering up like silver pencils, score on score,
> While surging millions hear the challenge come
> From microphones in communal canteens
> No right, no wrong, all's perfect, evermore[1]

Like many other architects of his period Farrell was seduced by the vision, and yet, and yet – there was always an undercurrent of doubt. His career to date shows all the evidence in microcosm of what has happened to modern architecture. He has been part of the great dégringolade.

When he returned from America and before he established an architectural practice in London, Farrell went to work for Colin Buchanan and Partners on a planning study for the city of Bath. If ever there was a city more likely to instill major doubts about the Modern Movement and to open the eyes of any architect to the virtues of pragmatism, formalism and collage it must be Bath. Working on the study to relieve the city of traffic concentrated the mind on the real problems of the interface between architecture and urban planning. It is later in his career that Farrell acknowledges these counter claims to straight Modern Movement development – first of all he has to build.

The establishment of the Farrell/Grimshaw partnership began with an important building that defined Farrell's attitude. The conversion of a 19th-century London terrace into a student hostel (1968) and the later Colonnades development of ten houses in London into 80 flats developed his philosophy of using buildings as a resource. This is one of Farrell's most important contributions to architectural thinking and practice. It is probably more important than his changing of architectural styles. He believes and practices the view that the city, like a good marriage, is a place for give and take. The older areas of our cities can either be wiped out by massive developments, or skilfully used in part as the collage of life. The most recent Mansion House Square project, (The Triangles, an alternative to the proposals by Mies van der Rohe) and his plans for Hammersmith Broadway show the particular skill of utilising what is there and adding to and improving it. It is a pragmatic approach which works. Farrell has the air of the old-fashioned family doctor who looks at the patient with gentle care and tries to cure his ills without drastic surgery. Like Alberti, who believed the house to be a small city and the city to be a large house, Farrell combines his gentle view of the city with a conviction that he can make space – new spaces from old ones. This is a great architectural gift. This approach has also made Farrell question many of the planning assumptions that govern so much British redevelopment. Do we need any new housing? During a period of economic recession architects should learn the value of exercising their design skills in the re-use of old

buildings. Pragmatism is a reaction in architectural terms to the Modern Movement's unerring demands for submission to the Zeitgeist. Pragmatic approaches to building problems mean that sometimes the old building is kept or adapted – not replaced by something that will itself soon be reflecting the past. One problem that any architect faces, working in the shadow of the demise of the kind of architecture that he was trained to build, is the need for a language that expresses this moment of transition.

It is doubtful whether the concept of Post-Modernism is an adequate substitute for a movement that was powered by politics as well as stylistic forces. Farrell's switch from hard-line, high-tech buildings designed with his partner Grimshaw to an adaptation of many of the American ideas about Post.Modernism to the British scene is what makes him a fascinating figure in the current debate. Because he is lucky enough to have considerable commercial expertise Farrell's practice has been able to develop and build a range of projects that expound in three dimensions the practice's approach to the world of architecture after modernism.

Farrell is always interested in what happens next. This has made him constantly aware of what other architects around the world are doing and had opened up his work to the charge that it is largely derivative. I do not think that this is entirely the case if the origins of the swing to Post-Modernism in Farrell's case is understood. It comes from his awareness of the needs of all those who build and those who look at buildings for a new architectural language. His language is based on an understanding of the contextual needs of a site as well as the need to make formal statements. Is he successful in his attempt to fuse art and utility? The weakness for any architect practising in the eighties is that the idea of architecture as an art has still to be fought for and accepted. This is particularly the case in parsimonious Thatcherite Britain where expediency is the password.

Forgetting for a moment the Terry Farrell who existed before 1980 (the year when he set up on his own), is it possible to define the Farrell Vision? It is a vision that has grown out of suffering. Breaking up a flourishing partnership is hard and inevitably damage will be caused to all parties. Farrell's anguish has also been over his approach to the art of architecture. The only way to be an artist is simply to become one, to make that decision and abandon all other pretensions. This is hard for an architect who has a particular skill at reconciling the needs of commerce and the city and has a reputation more for pragmatism than the uncompromising approach of the artist. I sense that Farrell is still tuning up his sensibilities. He is still comparatively young and has suffered from too many mundane commissions. There is a limit to how far the silk can be stretched over the sow's ear. What gives a critic and the world great confidence is that when Farrell had a major opportunity – his design for the Vauxhall Cross Competition – he produced a triumphant solution full of seeds of promise.

This design for offices and flats on the south bank of the Thames in London is masterly in its understanding of the grandeur and formality that can be achieved by the massing of classically-based pavilions on the river. The pedimented silhouettes of the buildings understood the beauty of shadows achieved in the low English light. Like Wren's City churches, this scheme depended upon a range of variations of the classical theme and an understanding of the London scale. There was nothing ad hoc about the Vauxhall scheme; it marked a break towards an understanding of formality. There are elements of this formality about the Water Treatment Centre in Reading – but there it is curiously compromised by the lack of context for such a statement.

Vauxhall Cross had a visionary quality about it that shows what Farrell is capable of on a large scale. It had about it, too, that sense of civic memory. There are hints of Art Deco, even of Shell Mex House, about it as well as an air of the 1930s' Walcott-like visions of the future of London. It is this growth of rational order from pragmatic tolerance that makes Farrell an architect with a major future.

Parallel with this developing interest in classical formality lies one other deeply English skill – an understanding of the picturesque. Work that Farrell has done on the Comyn Ching site in Covent Garden, London, is a sensitive understanding of the perpetual movement between space and form in architecture. In the same way that no artist drawing a still life can understand the forms without understanding the spaces around them, so Farrell utilised the spaces between and behind these Georgian buildings to free them for some new development. Elements of the new buildings illustrate the difficulties of finding new stylistic equivalents to the Georgian vernacular. I sense that Farrell is happy using the ordinary language of his surroundings and materials rather than, like Michael Graves for example, developing a new kind of symbolic language. Work on the house for the Jencks family in the late seventies gave Farrell a sense of the search that is current in that house for a new symbolism. It is Farrell's spatial virtuosity that comes to life in the Jencks house and utilises the relatively awkward older house as a source of spatial invention. The same skill applies in planning terms to the development for light industry at Wood Green where the planning diagram of buildings and courtyards gives as much space to the surrounding inner city area as it takes.

There is one quality about the work of this practice that is refreshing. Much of the work, particularly TV-am headquarters and the structures for Clifton Nurseries in London, have a sense of youthful entertainment about them – and God knows that is rare enough in contemporary architecture. The light-columns in Farrell's own office have this kind of jokiness derived as much from the skilled use of materials as the invention of new vocabulary.

How much of the change of heart of this architect has come about from public opinion? I think it fair to say that Farrell is one of the very few architects who are popular with the public. I think that this is due to his sharing of their concerns. He is interested in the protection of the urban environment and a development of its contextualism in his new buildings. He sees the point of decoration, although it has to be said that in artistic terms he has a long way to go, as do most contemporary architects. There is a danger in this populism because it can make an architect like Farrell into a responder rather than a creator. He has a slight over-enthusiasm for the application of styles as though they were advertisements. There can be no doubt about his willingness to acknowledge that the public is ahead of the profession. They have taken Modern Movement architecture in the way we used to take cod liver oil, only to find that it was not quite as good for us as we had hoped.

This is not the place for a detailed analysis of each of Farrell's buildings, it is the place to try to explore the context of his work. It is possible to see the movement, pushed by the public, away from doctrinaire modernism and a total belief in the values of technology to save our souls, to an understanding of the complex nature of the architect's dilemma. Today he has to adopt a multiplicity of approaches that will lead not to the survival of modern architecture but to the revival of the city and the real creation of spaces that we can use.

Farrell belongs with his contemporaries, like Jeremy Dixon and Piers Gough, who are relaxed about the gradual growth of a new architectural language. They are right not to panic – the growth of the new movement must be a gentle one that responds rather than imposes.

The buildings shown in detail in this monograph are only a beginning. Luckily and unluckily this is a practice that has a lot of commissions. It is important that they do not adapt their originality to commerce but show the world that the new architecture is developing serious roots. A lot of work can force the ideas too quickly into repetitive moulds – Farrell has shown a remarkable capacity for growth, but now is the time for a deeper artistic development. The next decade should reveal the inner depths behind the new clothes.

[1] John Betjeman, 'The Plannster's Vision' in New Bats and Old Belfries, John Murray, London 1945.

FARRELL MOVES TOWARDS SYMBOLISM
Charles Jencks

One of the less-quoted aphorisms of Mies was 'Build Don't Talk', a little-known saying perhaps because it didn't encourage the very medium by which it might be repeated. In Chicago this command amounted to something like censorship. Since there was so much opportunity to build, conversation about architecture never developed much beyond the appreciative grunt or the censorious groan. At least until Stanley Tigerman and The Chicago 7-11-18 appeared on the scene. In England, Leon Krier has made a new tradition (and modest trade) from the dictum 'Draw Don't Build', and the best architects such as James Stirling seem doomed to make a profession from the meagre average of one finished building per year. This paucity of British building leads, no doubt, to more and more elevated chat, a talk which is positively rococo in its intricate and obscure subtlety; and at the AA it can also lead to such drawing. It's all very beautiful, but it hasn't resulted yet in much exemplary building. Mainstream practice is largely unaffected. The best architects continue to miss the best commissions, a dolorous state of affairs which must be continuously deplored at every possible opportunity.

Against this cultural breakdown, the work of Terry Farrell gains in stature because it manages to bridge conventional stereotypes and traditional work patterns. He is an architect in the Chicago mould more given to building than to chat, but he has remained responsive to a changing theory while developing his own particular approach. This 'learning by doing' is perhaps more American than English, indebted to the pragmatic philosophy of John Dewey more than empiricism, just as Farrell's architecture develops from the Americans Kahn, Venturi, Stern and Graves. And this pragmatic approach has led to the accretion of practical knowledge: how to use new technologies in an expressive and economical way; how to exploit the best design talent in a medium-sized office; and how to knit together old and new buildings within a limited budget.

The approach might be partly summarised by the term 'Expedient Tech' — a phrase which has the advantage of being so ungainly that it is unlikely to be repeated. Expedient Tech was the earlier style of the Farrell/Grimshaw partnership. Not quite the transcendental High-Tech of Foster (which they criticised for being inflexible) nor the sleek packaging of mirrorplate builders, it obviously related to both approaches. Some obvious high points come to mind: the GRP bathroom pods of 1968, a built version of an Archigram speculation; the Park Road aluminium cladding which gave a new industrial image to housing in 1970 (now sadly aged without the compensating patina that might have formed on brick, copper or stone). More recently there is the doubly-curved polycarbonate sheeting used at Clifton Nurseries I — that wandering, undulating arch of green 'glass' that slithers over green plants — and the Teflon-coated, glass-reinforced fibre roof used at

1 Hector Guimard, Castel Béranger, Paris, 1894-8. The arch above the stepped-in rectangle sets curve against straight line. This flexible motif, allowing variation in height and width, is here intersected by columns at the extrados, the weak point. A formula which I developed into the 'face motif' and used to suggest eight different characters in a house is turned by Farrell at TV-am back towards its source at the Castel Béranger.

Clifton Nurseries II — a kind of buttoned-down-sailboat-tent with wire cables stretching taut to a green steel frame. It's a finely strung, post-tensioned Tuscan temple.

All of this Clever Tech might be applauded, and it certainly appeals to Martin Pawley and a host of born-again Modernists. When combined with fragments of the classical language it becomes canonic Post-Modernism, that is, doubly-coded and consciously aimed at different taste cultures. Yet the pragmatic approach to technique, organisation and city context does not in itself constitute an architecture, which must be a self-reflexive language, a discourse focused on the expressive plane itself. This is now in the process of formation.

The Non-Anxiety of Influence or Transformational Eclecticism

The sources of Farrell's Post-Modern Classicism are clear, and he is as candid as Robert Stern in admitting them. The Vauxhall project has the top and plinth of Graves' Portland building, transformed in certain ways to which we will return. Clifton Nurseries II modifies

107

Stern's fat columns and rusticated projects — notably the Llewelyn Park Poolhouse. The TV-am scheme mixes Venturian billboard with my own derivation of the Serliana, the ABA arch in the shape of a face with a stagger below it. This flexible motif is used as both a major gateway for cars and two side doors for pedestrians, a formula adapted, perhaps, not only from my own house but also Guimard's wonderful entrance to the Castel Béranger which also has columns smashing into the springing area of the arch. The Art Deco Classicism of Wall Street and the Chrysler Building, Streamline Moderne and Hollywood Deco are also apparent on the facade and plaza of TV-am.

But what of British influence? Aside from the Expedient Tech already mentioned there is little that Farrell finds of inspiration in the current scene. Mackintosh and Lutyens are, for him, the last great British masters from whom he can learn a free variation of classicism. The 'light' columns of his office show a Lutyensesque wit in their combination of column, quoin, lighting globe and heating duct. The influence of Mackintosh is apparent in the abstract rectilinear ornament, the flat horizontal, stepped mouldings, the setbacks and grids played against each other (as on the inside and outside of TV-am).

Admitting sources of inspiration is contrary to the Modernists' notion of creation ex nihilo and while creativity may indeed depend on intelligent theft inventively transformed, there is usually a taboo about admitting what an older generation considers a crime. Harold Bloom discusses this in a book which has itself influenced Vincent Scully and the American Post-Modernists (*The Anxiety of Influence, A Theory of Poetry*, 1973), and from this clarification we can understand more clearly the transfer of ideas and forms that is taking place. To quote Scully: '... Bloom's "strong poet", inevitably fastens on the work of his chosen precursor, purposely "misreads" it, and finally "swerves" from it to create a new field of action for his own design'.[1]

This 'swerving' from influence may be true when looked at from a psychological point of view, and it may help explain today's Mannerism, but in terms of the classical theory, it underscores the difference between imitating and copying . Imitation, the transformation of an idea and form through systematic recombination with other patterns, has always been encouraged by the classical tradition in opposition to replication, and this distinction finds an echo in TS Eliot's epigram: 'the bad poet borrows, the good poet steals'. Basically it's transformational eclecticism versus straight revivalism.

Note the way Farrell modifies several existing ideas on the facade of TV-am. Essentially a classical vocabulary of rustication and string courses is combined with an industrial vocabulary of corrugated metal and Art-Deco streamlines in polychromy. The base 'plinth' is in dark grey and black signifying night-time and dawn, while the lighter top in reds, yellows and oranges denotes the morning of breakfast television. The rusticated masonry and corrugated metal do not graduate in predictable diminution as in the classical palazzo (Michelozzo's Medici Palace, 1444, established this code). Rather they syncopate to the top AA, BB with the final stress C. This top and bottom emphasis sets the viewer on edge. A further tension is created by the illuminated 'keystone', a giant billboard which will become the logo for TV-am (and the letters can be faintly discerned in the trusswork).

This keystone seems straightforward at first: it has a normal proportion of splay and sides. But on further inspection it turns out to be a distorted and transformed motif, combined first with a lightweight truss (to lower wind loads), secondly with a cathode tube (to light up the bisected centre), thirdly with 'organ-pipe' decoration, and fourthly with side string courses or streamlines. In effect it becomes still a fifth thing, the morning sunburst. The facade is then a creative transformation of several influences combined for the symbolic role of advertising breakfast television, as well as a welcoming sign, an archway for the car. As a whole it oscillates between one context and the next, always avoiding the cliché that the replication promotes. But for this very reason it may cause offence to some people. Traditionalists might term it a pastiche, as they tend to term a transformation of classical masonry into steel and glass; Modernists will be annoyed by the recognisable keystone, Purists by the hybrid language. Farrell may then have to pay the price which creative transformation and crossing traditions often entail: the accusations of ugliness and vulgarity. One might recall in this respect 19th-century cases — JJ Lequeu, William Burges, Robert Kerr, JC Loudon — where a symbolic architecture has also led to such censure, and remark that then it was defended as having 'muscularity', 'character' and 'truthfulness'. With time I presume Farrell's archway will be appreciated as an imaginative synthesis in a Free-Style Classicism.

Abstraction and Representation

One of the reasons why the facade has its openwork configuration is cost. The front wall, originally in glass, came in at a bid of £240,000 and more than £100,000 had to be trimmed from this figure. The solution was a lightweight truss to avoid wind loads, a cheaper material — corrugated metal — and a Venturian 'Billdingboard', a thin facade that shows its true nature at both ends (where further symbols occur). Economy often forces an architect to concentrate his mind on essentials: it made Graves simplify the facade and interior of his Portland Building so that it came in six million dollars cheaper than his competitors, and here it has focused Farrell's mind in simplifying details and re-using as much of the pre-existing building as possible. On the expressive plane it may force the architect from representation to abstraction. On the interior of TV-am, for instance, two grey grids are used on the ceiling at the same height, a very simple, cheap abstraction

2 Michelozzo, Pallazzo Medici-Riccardi, Florence, 1444-64. Then gradation of stonework from heavy bottom to light top was formulated in this building and established the typical code of the rusticated facade. A feeling of greater height is created by gradation; each floor is accentuated and the symbolism of usage is underscored (public base, piano nobile, private attic etc). Farrell's rustication of TV-am also observes the basic heavy/light distinction while adding a sun symbolism.

3 Elevation of TV-am shows the rustication of the top five sections having a complex rhythm that stresses top and bottom in a syncopated manner.

which pulls together the different spaces and gives a cool grey indirect light.

There is another, more important way in which representational imagery is made abstract: by multivalence, ambiguity and by interweaving several images at once so they afford multiple meanings. We have just touched on this in the TV-am archway, the multiple image which avoids its easy unities, its 'flash' qualities, by displacing them with further meaning, above all technical ones. One problem with Art Deco has always been its glitsy ease, its playing to the crowd. One can sense such a populist streak in Farrell's work but it is, by and large, overcome by the multivalence of images.

A negative case where this may not be true is the back of TV-am, where breakfast TV 'eggs' will decorate a syncopation of arches and staggers; the success or otherwise of this back elevation may depend on the final complexity and synthesis of motifs. An ambiguous case, which seems to work out in part, is the swag motif on the Clifton Nurseries II: here real, natural swags are suspended between decorative 'ears'. They recall Labrouste's garlands at the Bibliothèque Sainte-Geneviève, as well as Peter Smithson and David van Zanten's recent comments on swaggery (as stemming

from a ritual application of nature turned into symbolic decoration). At Clifton II the game consists in reversing history since the swags are real garlands. This clever reinterpretation does a lot to displace the explicit imagery, but one may still have doubts as to whether the 'ears' and 'diglyphs' are not too stressed.

Such extreme representation stems from iconic architecture, again Lequeu, and Pop art. Whether it is appropriate in Covent Garden is arguable. The Tuscan temple of Inigo Jones, St Pauls, which acted as the major pretext for Farrell's Tuscan half-temple, is of course a sober affair with its plain heavy proportions and vernacular roof. Before the Clifton Nurseries were decorated with ears, swags and the rest, it had a quiet dignity, the abstraction which gave its simple message a weight and *gravitas*. The presence of the Teflon roof and green steel structure added seriousness to the building. Now it has been transformed in a picturesque and whimsical direction, a direction which may have always been intended if one judges by the earliest drawings. Nonetheless I find it a loss, the ascendancy of representation over abstraction. The difficulty and challenge of symbolism is in the careful balance of implicit and explicit sign; and this can be achieved by making explicit meanings multivalent, and thereby abstract.

The Return to a New Tradition

No doubt Post-Modern Classicism, in its first years of life, has all the teething problems of early Modernism: diagrammatic exaggeration, awkwardness, leaky roofs, naivety. Perhaps freshness mitigates these drawbacks, if it doesn't altogether excuse them. On the inside of TV-am, Farrell will attempt a symbolic ordering which may seem a trifle ingenuous: to the East of the plaza will be a Japanese temple, in the Near East a ziggurat stair will be built, and to the West some Dallas mirrorplate and Hollywood palms. Undoubtedly this will go down rather well with Peter Jay, David Frost and those producers who see their message as having global implications, but one might ask whether the imagery might not have more complex ramifications. Perhaps it will when finally built.

In any case, it seems to me that the most mature statement of Farrell's work is his Vauxhall scheme, a proposition which won't be built. This was conceived in March 1982 when Farrell was locked up in a hospital, with a collapsed lung, far away from the hustle and bustle of his office. It resulted from a competition, called by the Minister of the Environment, to overcome the problem of the 'Green Giant', a commercial leviathan originally proposed for the site south of Vauxhall Bridge. Farrell's scheme reached the last stage of the competition only to be displaced, under the developer's influence, Arunbridge, in favour of a scheme rather like a late sixties megastructure. The introduction of public opinion, if not participation, turned out to be farcical. After voting on their favourite (either the Lacey or Farrell design) they were cheated of knowing their choice. Whatever the final outcome of this low comedy, the Farrell entry shows a competent authority, a sure transformation of classical themes, including those of Michael Graves. In this sense it represents a return to a tradition which is, paradoxically, new.
There are four basic transformations of a single idea.

The smallest riverside flats are given a four-square volume rather like Ledoux's masterful solution to the same problem type (the *Grange parée*). Ledoux cuts a centre void between two towers and supports this with a gentle pitched roof. Farrell adds wings to his version and thus defines garden paths to each side.

Behind these low-rise high-cost flats is a palace of apartments with a U-shape plan and a luxury penthouse — also with a pitched roof. Thus the unidirectional block in front is transformed into a more complex chateau type of plan. Finally, in the office blocks, the U-shape becomes two slabs connected by a bridge — or an H-shape block squashed down so that, as elsewhere, almost every room has a view of the river.

One of the hidden aspects of the Thames is that it suggests a front and back to any nearby building. Farrell accepts this latent rule and turns it into an image. His model shows row upon row of theatre-goers gazing over each others' shoulders to watch the world float by, an explicit celebration of the Thames in a rather Venetian manner. The directionality of the 'faces' is imposed by the broken pediments and the volumes which are sometimes staggered like theatre seats. The four different broken or set-back pediments (containing boardrooms or double-height living space) correspond to the four variations on a theme.

What gives the proposal strength, and I would even say brilliance, is the interlocking manner in which these parts are slotted together. The result is a pulsating, urban space of variety, a complex pattern of positive and negative volume which is repetitive and ambiguous at the same time. Like a geometric quilt which has been programmed with three or four conflicting patterns at once, the invention sparks off various readings. They are reminiscent of current contextual work, of Krier's urbanism, of Bofill's palaces; more to the point, they

4 Henri Labrouste, Bibliothèque Sainte-Geneviève, Paris, 1838-50). Stone swags partly used to soften an austere image, partly meant to symbolise an ancient ritual celebration — decorating buildings with garlands during feast days, marriages, spring festivals and so on.

5 Clifton Nurseries II with its real swags, some of which are for sale. Note the way the false facade screens the car parking from the main square — a welcome urban function.

6 Terry Farrell Partnership, Vauxhall Bridge competition entry, 1982.

7 Thomas Jefferson, 'Academical Village', University of Virginia, Charlottesville, Va, 1816-26. A subtle interlocking of ten pavilions for professors, student rooms (along the colonnade), gardens and 'hotels' (for eating) in back and a network of services and smaller buildings. The careful variations on a simple theme, both in elevation and section, produce a controlled layout which is always full of surprise.

are reminiscent of Thomas Jefferson's 'academical village' in Charlottesville, Virginia. Farrell's intention was to evolve a new village/city typology by varying a basic building block in plan and scale. Unfortunately it won't be realised at Vauxhall; but it is unlikely to remain lost for long, given the deep concern in this office for getting ideas built.

Postscript: A Note on Our Collaboration

In late 1978 Maggie Keswick and I began to work with Terry Farrell on reconstructing a nineteenth-century house we had recently bought in London (illustrated on pages 52-55). We had already worked out a preliminary scheme, but after consulting a structural surveyor had decided we needed the resources of an office and of a flexible, experienced architect to help us work it through and build it. I had asked Terry to lecture at the AA and at a RIBA meeting on (his title) 'Buildings as a Resource', and these talks had shown his skills at recycling old buildings (while consulting the inhabitants) and producing High-Tech, economical details. For over two and a half years we worked together on the shell and spaces of the house with Terry contributing particularly in such areas as the central staircase, the study annexe and the top attic. Four of us would meet together for mutual design sessions and this collaboration proved especially fruitful when we all contributed ideas from our own special concerns. With the 'sun-stair', for instance, the structural concept was worked out by Terry (helped by the engineer David French), the visual and symbolic design was done by me, the functional aspect by Maggie and details by David Quigley succeeded by Simon Sturgis, a designer in Farrell's office. It was David who noticed there could be 52 steps, one for each week of the year which suggested their further division into seven parts. Meantime I realised how the building moulds for the concrete steps — the fact there were three different ones — could be used to fabricate different sun rays, rays which would pulsate (when seen from underneath). Terry kept control of the structural and constructional parameters and would suggest and develop the areas open for choice. This work and its positive conclusion supported my belief in participation in design: that collaboration can be synergetic. Further work by other craftsmen and an artist on the stair-rail and mosaic confirmed this belief since, like us, they became involved in the idea behind the design. After collaborating with other artists and designers over five years (the time it took to complete the house) I have come to believe that participation is most fruitful when there is a strong organising idea, and that this role is best served by a symbolic programme or some credible goal towards which various specialists can work.

Whilst Terry had an influence on the house, we perhaps had an influence on his work. His general shift to Post-Modernism, or at least his divergence from his former partner Nick Grimshaw, was in some degree a result of our collaboration. And his interest in symbolism, the subject of this article, particularly his design of metaphorical elements related to the body, and his 'light columns' (already mentioned) spring from our joint design sessions. I was at this time (1978-82) trying to see the ultimate limits of a representational architecture and had many students designing symbolic columns which were technically and functionally motivated. The results were extreme enough to force some of us in a more abstract direction, in fact towards 'abstract representation' as I was to later call it. How much of these arguments Terry found useful is not for me to say, but we were influential in one pragmatic way, being responsible for his introduction to the Clifton Nurseries client. Jacob Rothschild, the owner of Clifton, has taken an interest in new design ideas, which is rare for someone in his position. When the history of Modernism and Post-Modernism comes to be written, the relative dearth of clients supporting new architecture in Great Britain — of whatever brand — will become clear. Only a very few corporate and public clients and Palumbo, Rothschild and Sainsbury (to name three) have had the courage to support architecture as an art. Experiment in architecture, speculating on a new urbanism, ornament and symbolism that are more than revivalist, has been mostly on paper, or in books. Post-Modernism has yet to flourish in England. Farrell's determination to build in this climate (of opinion) is thus all the more to be respected and admired.

8 Sunwell in the Thematic House: The focus of the symbolic programme of the sun at the centre of four seasons; looking up. The sunwell was the result of a fruitful collaboration. Farrell worked out the structural and planning concepts of an integrated cylinder/stairtread. I worked out the visual design of the stairtreads and their pulsation rhythms. David Quigley noted the number of 52 treads and we jointly designed the seven vertical divisions (he also designed the two concrete 'faces' visible here). Maggie worked on the functional aspects of its location and use; I designed the stair-rail and, with Eduardo Paolozzi, worked on his mosaic of the Black Hole which fills the central circle at the bottom (not visible).

Notes

1 Vincent Scully, *The Shingle Style Today or the Historian's Revenge*, New York, 1974, p.2.

This essay originally appeared in *Architectural Design* special profile *British Architecture*, London 1982, pp.194-5.

BIBLIOGRAPHY

General articles by Terry Farrell

'The Louis Kahn Studio at the University of Pennsylvania, *Arena*, March 1967

'A Designer's Approach to Rehabiliation — Three Inner London Cases', Chapter 5 of *Building Conversion and Rehabiliation: Design for Change in Building Use*, Thomas A Markus (Ed.), Newnes-Butterworth 1979

'Design Matters', monthly column in *RIBA Journal*, April-December 1983

'Michael Graves: Building and Projects 1966-1981' (book review) *Building*, 2 September 1981

Conference Papers

'The Making of an Architect', York Schools of Architecture Conference (unpublished)

Hull RIBA Conference, 'Architecture: Opportunities and Achievements', 1976.

FARRELL/GRIMSHAW PARTNERSHIP

General articles about the practice

'Setting Up In Practice', *Architects' Journal*, January 1971

'The Men Most Likely To', *Building Design*, 25 February 1972

Farrell/Grimshaw: Recent Work, *Architectural Design*, February 1973

Survival by Design: RIBA Lecture — Architects' Approach to Architecture, *RIBA Journal*, October 1974

Buildings As A Resource, Architectural Association Lecture, *RIBA Journal*, May 1976

'Whatever Happened To The Systems Approach', *Architectural Design*, May 1979

TERRY FARRELL PARTNERSHIP

Selected articles about the practice

'Pragmatic Classicism', *Domus*, July 1981

'Reflections on Farrell', *Architects Journal*, 19 August 1981

'Best Products — Lateral Thinking', *Architects Journal*, 25 November 1981

'Attitudes of an Anglo-Saxon', *Architects Journal*, 10 November 1982

'The Man Who Took High Tech Out To Play', *Sunday Times* Magazine, 16 January 1983

'Farrell Moves Towards Symbolism' by Charles Jencks plus Terry Farrell Partnership work, *British Architecture*, Academy Editions 1982

LIST OF BUILDINGS AND PROJECTS

Between 1965 and 1980 all works indicated by an asterisk (*) were executed in partnership with Nicholas Grimshaw.

1968 Hostel for overseas students*	Paddington, London
1970 Forty Co-Ownership Flats*	Regent's Park, London
1973 Runneymede Warehouse*	Runneymede, England
1974-76 The Colonnades urban redevelopment*	Paddington, London
1975 Rehabilitation study of 1,000 older* council-owned dwellings	Westminster, London
1976 Herman Miller Factory*	Bath, England
1979 BMW Distribution Centre*	Bracknell, England
1979-81 Digital Factory conversion*	Reading, England
1979-80 Clifton Nurseries Greenhouse I Garden Centre and Shop	Bayswater, London
1980-81 Clifton Nurseries II Garden Shop and Public Park	Covent Garden, London
1974-81 Low-Cost Timber Frame Housing for Maunsel Housing Society* and Warrington New Town	Greater London and Warrington, England
1979-81 Urban Infill Factories	Wood Green, London
1980-81 Architects' Own Offices	Marylebone, London
1980-81 Crafts Council Gallery and Information Centre	Waterloo Place, London
1979-80 Private House	Holland Park, London
1980-81 Alexandra Pavilion	Haringey, London

1 Clifton Nurseries, Bayswater 1979-80   2 Private House 1979-80

3 Clifton Nurseries II, Covent Garden 1980-81

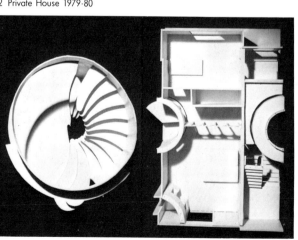

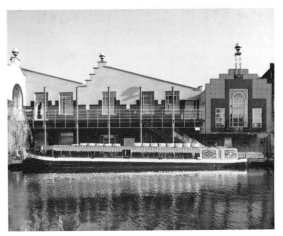

4 Alexandra Pavilion 1980-81

5 Vauxhall Cross Competition 1982

6 Television Broadcasting Centre 1981-82

1982 Festival Exhibition Building	Liverpool, England
1979-82 Water Treatment Centre	Reading, England
1982 Vauxhall Cross National Competition	Vauxhall, London
1981-82 Private house for Jacob Rothschild and family	St John's Wood, London
1981-82 Television Broadcasting Centre	Camden, London
1982-83 Radio Headquarters	Portland Place, London
1982-83 Television Studios	West India Docks, London
1984 The Triangles. Mansion House	The City of London
1978-85 Mixed Development of a Historic Triangular Island Site	Covent Garden, London
1982-85 Banking Building	The City of London
1983-86 Offices and Bank	The City of London
1982-84 Workshop and Offices	Chiswick, London
1983-85 Clubhouse Headquarters and Boat Store	Henley, England
1983-85 Piazza di Putney, Station Remodelling	Putney, London
1984 Redevelopment Study for Transport Interchange on Island Site	Hammersmith, London
1980-85 Two Adjoining Corner Office Buildings	Reading, London

7 Private House 1981-82

8 Piazza di Putney 1983-85

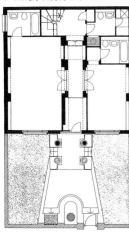

ACKNOWLEDGEMENTS

The wide range of building types undertaken by the office of Terry Farrell, and the complexity of solutions adopted, relies not only on traditional group team-work but to an unusual extent upon the creative contribution of individual architectural office has conventionally related methodical and disciplined teamwork to narrowly defined architectural goals; but an office with broad and 'inclusive' aims positively engages and indeed needs a wide range of creative contributions. The following are the main participants in the work from 1980-1983.

Ken Allinson, Page Ayres, Laurence Bain, Neil Bennett, John Chatwin, David Clarke, Jim Corcoran, Andrew Cowan, Michael Donovan, Craig Downie, Susan Farrell, Joe Foges, Michael Glass, Andrew Hobson, Simon Hudspith, Steve Ibbotson, Peter Jenkins, John Langley, Martin Lazenby, Colin Leisk, John Letherland, Caroline Lwin, Steve Marshall, Jonathan McDowell, Alan Morris, Satish Patel, Jeremy Peacock, John Petrarca, Neil Porter, David Quigley, Nicholas Rank, Thierry Reinhardt, Oliver Richards, Doug Smith, Steve Smith, Richard Solomon, Doug Streeter, Simon Sturgis, Peter Tigg, Kim Ward, Geoff Warn, Clive Wilkinson, Gary Young.

Each project has a designated job architect (indicated by an asterisk in each project's credits in this monograph) whose task it is to provide continuity through all phases of the work and to co-ordinate the in-house team as well as the various consultants. Terry Farrell leads on all matters of design and policy for each project and his partner, John Chatwin, who has worked with Terry Farrell now for over twelve years, brings to each project his highly valued organisational skills, his quiet wisdom and his care and concern for architecture.

Within the office it has been John Langley's task to assemble, co-ordinate and do the detailed design and layout of this monograph.

PHOTOGRAPHIC CREDITS

Academy Editions, p.12 (5); Aerofilms Ltd, p.1 (3), p.78 (17); Alsop, Barnett and Lyall, p.11 (4); Archigram, p.16 (10); British Tourist Authority, p.11 (3); Richard Bryant, p.2, p.6, p.16 (11), p.47 (4,5), p.50 (15), p.51 (16-18), p.61 (2,4), p.62 (5-7), p.63 (8), p.65 (11-13), p.73 (lower), p.3&4 (7,8,10,11), p.5&6 (12-16), p.7 (17), p.82 (A), p.83 (B-E), p.85 (5), p.86 (A-C), p.87 (D-F), p.90 (A-E), p.91 (F-H); Graham Challifour, p.35 (15), p.38 (10-14), p.39 (15,17,18), p.51 (19), p.58 (7), p.66 (5); Martin Charles, p.12 (6), p.13 (8); Craig Downie, p.101(5); Paul Farrell, p.7 (19); Terry Farrell, p.18 (2), p.19 (3-5), p.21 (8); Joe Foges, p.100 (3); Andrew Holmes, p.20 (6); Charles Jencks, p.107 (1), p.109 (2-3), p.110 (4-5), p.111 (7); Bob Kirkman, p.70 (11), p.111 (6); John Langley, p.48 (5-6), p.49 (7-8); Ralph Lerner and Richard Reid, p.10 (1); Rex Lowden, p.33 (13); James Mortimer p.46 (1,3), p.48 (7); Satish Patel, p.54 (6,7), p.55 (8-10), p.59 (9), p.67 (8), p.73 (upper), p.77 (7), p.79 (18-22); p.104 (1); Alberto Piovano, p.72 (1), p.3&4 (9); Portmerion, p.11 (2); Cedric Price, p.15 (9); Joe Reid and John Peck, p.13 (7), p.18 (1), p.26 (11-13), p.27 (14-17), p.31 (5-7), p.33 (11,12), p.34 (14), p.36 (1-5), p.42 (5-7), p.43 (8,9), p.44 (10-12), p.45 (14,15), p.49 (13), p.57 (1,4), p.58 (5,6); Heini Schneebeli, p.112 (8); Patrick Shanahan, p.59 (8,10); Tim Street-Porter, p.24 (1); TFP, p.24 (2-4), p.25 (7-10), p.48 (8,9), p.49 (11,12), p.52 (1-3), p.7 (18), p.74 (39), p.81 (33-38), p.84 (3,4), p.100 (3), p.101 (5); Tessa Traeger, p.25 (5,6)

Résumé

Cette monographie présente les réalisations et les projets de l'un des architectes les plus importants de Grand-Bretagne, Terry Farrell. Elle a été préparée en collaboration avec la Terry Farrell Partnership et contient quatre essais, dont deux écrits par l'architecte lui-même, qui situent l'oeuvre dans son contexte.

Dans son essai, 'L'architecture britannique après le modernisme', Farrell se penche sur le développement de l'architecture en Grande-Bretagne depuis le début des années 60, et il évoque les problèmes de changement d'identité culturelle et l'état actuel — et futur — de l'architecture britannique après le modernisme. 'Le modernisme etait centralisateur, il avait comme idéologie le "style international". L'opposition est d'origine régionale et les centres dispersés qui émergent sont le fruit d'architectes contemporains qui donnent une expression à leur culture, comme le font Graves, Krier, Botta, Hollein, Bofill et Isozaki. Le modernisme était impersonnel, une architecture de l'anonymat; la contre-réaction donne la préférence à des architectes dont les visions et le talent sont éminemment personnels. L'esthétique de la machine sans décoration fait de la place à la décoration et à l'ornement; le dynamisme masculin est remplacé par la sensualité et la sensibilité; l'extrême simplification rationalisée par la complexité et la contradiction; le futurisme par l'historicisme; et l'universalité des solutions par la contextualité. Les Britanniques finiront peut-être par découvrir qu'un style plus libre 'd'après le modernisme' est tout à fait leur genre d'architecture, du fait de ses qualités typiquement britanniques, représentées par une approche tolérante, éclectique, contextuelle, plus romantique et plus ouverte.'

Farrell note qu'en ce qui le concerne sa croyance en une philosophie centralisatrice et sa fascination pour la technologie en tant que telle ont cédé la place à une préoccupation quant à la qualité de la vie et une pratique de l'architecture plus libre et plus joyeuse. Dans l'essai autobiographique du même nom, Farrell fair référence à la parabole du hérisson et du renard d'Isaiah Berlin pour illustrer son développement personnel depuis l'époque de ses études à Newcastle et à Philadelphie jusqu'à l'heure actuelle, c'est-à-dire son évolution du fondamentalisme enseigné par Kahn à son éclectisme radical actuel. Ceci se termine par un essai illustré sur le rôle primordial de la silhouette humaine comme générateur de la forme en architecture.

Les constructions et les projets mentionnés appartiennent principalement à la très courte période d'indépendance de Farrell au sein de la Terry Farrell Partnership, à part une récapitulation du travail entrepris en association avec Nicholas Grimshaw entre 1965 et 1980. Ce sont des logements, des bâtiments industriels, des studios, des bureaux et des pavillons en verre; ils représentent toute une gamme d'interventions dans le domaine de l'architecture, allant de la conservation et de la remise en état jusqu'à la construction du neuf. Chaque bâtiment ou projet est accompagné d'une documentation complète, comprenant les dessins de présentation, quelques croquis conceptuels, et des photographies en couleurs et en noir et blanc ayant fait l'objet de commandes spéciales.

Dans 'Art pragmatique et virtuosité spatiale', Colin Amery émet l'opinion que Farrell appartient à cette race particulière d'architectes britanniques qui, ayant reçu une formation anglaise traditionnelle basée sur les sources classiques, se sont ensuite inspirés de la vision américaine d'un monde d'après-guerre dominé par la technologie. D'après Amery, la carrière de Farrell, jusqu'à ce jour, représente en miniature l'évolution de l'architecture moderne. Dans l'exploration biographique qui suit, Amery déclare que la philosophie d'un architecte qui se sert des bâtiments comme matière première est 'une des contributions les plus importantes de Farrell dans le domaine de la réflexion et de la pratique en architecture'. Une approche pragmatique nuancée des quartiers plus anciens des villes est en effet manifeste dans les projets les plus récents (le square de Mansion House et Hammersmith); ce pragmatisme est une réaction contre la soumission du mouvement moderne au *Zeitgeist*. Grâce à sa considérable expertise commerciale, le groupe de Farrell a pu développer et construire une gamme de projets qui expriment en trois dimensions l'attitude du groupe dans le domaine de l'architecture après le modernisme.

Le langage de Farrell est basé sur la compréhension des besoins contextuels d'un site et aussi sur un besoin de fair des déclarations formelles. Prenant l'exemple 'décisif' du concours de Vauxhall Cross, Amery essaye de définir la vision de Farrell — lorsqu'on lui donne la possibilité de travailler sur une grande échelle — parce que là se manifeste 'le développement de l'ordre rationnel à partir de la tolérance pragmatique, qui fait de Farrell un architecte de très grand avenir.' Deux autres projets, à savoir Comyn Ching et la maison de Jencks, dénotent l'un et l'autre une compréhension du pittoresque et de la virtuosité spatiale, ainsi qu'une utilisation du langage ordinaire du contexte et la recherche d'un nouveau langage symbolique. Ces projets sont empreints d'une autre qualité rafraîchissante, rare en architecture contemporaine; un air de jeunesse et d'amusement. Farrell fait partie des rares architectes aimés du public, parce qu'il partage ses préoccupations, qu'il protège l'environnement urbain, et qu'il développe l'importance du contexte urbain dans les nouveaux bâtiments qu'il construit. Farrell, ainsi que ses contemporains Jeremy Dixon et Piers Gough, appartient à un nouveau mouvement au langage architectural nouveau.

Dans son essai, 'Farrell s'oriente vers le symbolism', Charles Jencks explore les sources du classicisme post-moderne de Farrell, qui a remplacé le style tech ingénieux ou opportun que le caractérisait auparavant. Utilisant la notion littéraire d'angoisse à propos d'influence, Jencks démontre que les références de Farrell au travail d'autres architectes sont le fait d'un éclectisme transformationnel plutôt que d'un revivalisme proprement dit.

L'édifice de TV-am, et particulièrement sa clef de voûte, est donné comme exemple d'une synthèse pleine d'imagination dans un classicisme de style libre.

Dans une analyse plus détaillée de ces projets, Jencks évoque les raisons du passage de la représentation à l'abstraction dans le travail de Farrell et la multivalence qui en résulte. Le projet de Vauxhall, 'la formulation la plus mûre de l'oeuvre de Farrell . . . fait preuve d'une autorité compétente dans le remaniement des thèmes classiques.' Jencks poursuit: 'Ce qui donne du caractère à cette proposition, et je dirais même un côte spectaculaire, c'est la manière dont les différentes parties sont emboîtées les unes dans les autres. Il en résulte un espace urbain varié, qui palpite, un arrangement complexe de volumes positifs et négatifs, à la fois répétitif et ambigu. A la manière d'un assemblage géométrique programmé sur la base de trois ou quatre dessins conflictuels, cette invention déclenche plusiers lectures. Ces projets sont dans la ligne du travail contextuel actuel: que ce soit l'urbanisme de Krier ou les palais de Bofill; ou bien plutôt, ils font penser au 'village académique' de Thomas Jefferson à Charlottesville, en Virginie. L'intention de Farrell était de développer une nouvelle typologie village/ville en variant le pâté de maison de base, dans le plan et dans l'échelle. Ce ne sera malheureusement pas réalisé à Vauxhall; cela ne risque guère d'être perdu pour longtemps, étant donnée la détermination du groupe de Farrell à faire construire des idées.'

En post-scriptum, l'auteur rapporte leur collaboration de deux ans et demi à la maison de Jencks et l'influence que ceci a eu sur leurs idées.

On trouve enfin une liste complète des bâtiments et des projets ainsi qu'une bibliographie.

Zusammenfassung

Diese Architekturmonographie stellt Gebäude und Projekte des führenden britischen Architekten Terry Farrell vor, und wurde in Zusammenarbeit mit der Terry Farrell Teilhaberschaft angefertigt. Sie enthält vier Essays, zwei davon vom Architekten selbst, die sein Werk im Kontext zeigen.

In seinem Aufsatz über 'Die britische Architektur nach dem Modernismus', reflektiert Farrell auf Entwicklungen der Praxis der Architektur in Grossbritannien seit den frühen sechziger Jahren und diskutiert Probleme des Wandels und der kulturellen Identität sowie den Zustand und die Zukunft der britischen Architektur nach dem Modernismus. 'Der Modernismus war zentralisierend, seine Ideologie der "Internationale Stil". Die Gegenbewegungen dazu sind regional, und die zutage tretenden dispersen Zentren werden von zeitgenössischen, ihre Kultur ausdrückenden Architekten wie Graves, Krier, Botta, Hollein, Bofill und Isozaki erhellt. Der Modernismus war unpersönlich, eine Architektur der Anonymität; die Gegenreaktion darauf hebt Architekten mit höchst persönlichen architektonischen Vorstellungen und Fähigkeiten hervor. Auf die schmucklose Maschinenästhetik wird mit Dekoration und Ornament reagiert; auf männlichen Trieb mit Sinnlichkeit und Sensibilität; auf rationalistische Übersimplifizierung mit Komplexität und Widerspruch; auf Futurismus mit Historizismus und auf die Universalität der Lösungsmöglichkeiten mit Kontextualität. Schliesslich mögen die Briten entdecken, dass ein eher freistilhafter 'Nachmodernismus' die ihnen weitgehend entsprechende Architekturform ist, einfach, weil sie in ihrem toleranten, eklektischen kontextuellen, romantischeren und offeneren Zugang so britisch ist.'

Farrell sieht in seiner eigenen Erfahrung einen Aufbruch weg vom Glauben an eine zentralisierende Philosophie und vom Faszinosum der Technologie um ihrer selbst willen zu einer Beschäftigung mit der Qualität des Lebens und einer freieren und fröhlicheren Praxis in der Architektur hin.
In dem ebenso betitelten autobiographischen Essay gebraucht Farrell Isaiah Berlins Idee vom Igel und dem Fuchs, um seine persönliche Entwicklung von der Studienzeit in Newcastle und Philadelphia bis zur Gegenwart zu erläutern, das heisst, ideologisch vom Fundamentalismus, den ihn Kahn lehrte, zu seinem heutigen radikalen Eklektizismus. Er schliesst mit einem illustrierten Aufsatz über das Thema der menschlichen Gestalt als wichtigster Erzeugerin architektonischer Form.

Die dargestellten Gebäude und Projekte sind auf die sehr kurze Zeitspanne der unabhängigen Arbeit Farrells in der Terry Farrell Teilhaberschaft konzentriert, jedoch wird auch eine Zusammenfassung der Arbeit geliefert, die in der Partnerschaft mit Nicholas Grimshaw 1965-1980 enstand. Diese umfasst Wohnhäuser. Industriegebäude, Ateliers, Büro- und Ausstellungsgebäude und führt eine Bandbreite architektonischer Interventionen vor, die Erhaltung und Wiederherstellung ebenso wie Neubau einbezieht. Jedes Gebäude oder Projekt wird vollständig mit Zeichnungen, gelegentlichen konzept-

ionellen Skizzen und zu diesem Zweck in Auftrag gegebenen Farb- und Schwarzweissphotographien dokumentiert.

Colin Amery sieht Farrell in seiner Schrift über 'Pragmatische Kunst und räumliche Virtuosität' als einem besonderen Schlag britischer Architekten zugehörig, deren Ausbildung sowohl das traditionell englische, auf klassischem Ursprung beruhende als auch das von der amerikanischen Vision einer hochtechnisierten Nachkriegswelt inspirierte Studium umfasst. Er weist darauf hin, dass Farrells Karriere bis heute mikrokosmisch all das, was in der modernen Architektur geschehen ist, aufweist. In der nun folgenden biographischen Untersuchung beschreibt Amery die Philosophie des Architekten, Gebäude als Hilfsmittel zu gebrauchen, als 'einen von Farrells wichtigsten Beiträgen zu architektonischer Praxis.' Die jüngsten Projekte (Mansion House Square und Hammersmith) zeigen einen sanft pragmatischen Zugang zu den älteren Teilen der Städte, das heisst Pragmatismus als Reaktion auf die Unterwerfung der modernen Bewegung unter den *Zeitgeist*. Wegen seines bemerkenswerten kommerziellen Geschicks konnte Farrells Büro eine Reihe von Projekten entwerfen und bauen, die die Einstellung des Büros zur Welt der Architektur nach dem Modernismus im Dreidimensionalen erläutern.

Farrells Sprache beruht auf dem Verständnis der sich aus dem Zusammenhang ergebenden Bedürfnisse eines Bauplatzes ebenso wie auf dem Bedürfnis, formale Aussagen zu machen. Indem er das 'meisterhafte' Beispiel des Vauxhall Cross Wettbewerbs benutzt, sucht Amery Farrells Vorstellung zu definieren, wenn ihm die Gelegenheit gegeben wird, in grossem Massstab zu arbeiten, da es das 'Anwachsen der rationalen Ordnung von der pragmatischen Toleranz auszeigt, das Farrell zu einem Architekten mit grosser Zukunft macht.' Zwei weitere Projekte, Comyn Ching und das Haus der Jencks, zeigen ein Verständnis der jeweils malerischen und räumlichen Virtuosität, des Gebrauchs der herkömmlichen Sprache des Kontexts und die Suche nach einer neuen symbolhaften Sprache. Eine weiters erfrischende Qualität der Arbeit ist ein Sinn für jugendliche Unterhaltsamkeit, der in der zeitgenössischen Architektur selten ist. Farrell ist einer der wenigen Architekten, der bei der Öffentlichkeit beliebt ist, weil er ihre Sorgen teilt, die städtische Umgebung schützt und ihren Zusammenhang in neuen Gebäuden weiterentwickelt. Farrell zählt, mit seinen Zeitgenossen Jeremy Dixon und Piers Gough, zu einer neuen Bewegung mit einer neuen architektonischen Sprache.

Charles Jencks untersucht in seinem Essay 'Farrell auf dem Weg zum Symbolismus' die Ursprünge von Farrells postmodernem Klassizismus, der seinen früheren 'geschickten' und 'zweckmässigen' 'Tech'-Stil abgelöst hat. Den literarischen Begriff von der Angst vor Beeinflussung benutzend, zeigt Jencks, dass Farrells Zitate der Arbeit anderer Architekten im Gegensatz zu einfacher Wiederbelebung einen transformierenden Eklektizismus beinhalten. TV-am und insbesondere sein Schlussstein wird als Beispiel

einer phantasievollen Synthese in freistilhaftem Klassizismus benutzt.

In einer detaillierteren Analyse der Projekte diskutiert Jencks die Gründe für eine Wendung von der Darstellung zur Abstraktion und der daraus sich ergebenden Multivalenz in Farrells Arbeit. Das Vauxhall-projekt, 'die reifste Manifestation der Arbeit Farrells . . . zeigt kompetente Autorität, die sichere Umwandlung klassischer Themen.' Jencks fährt fort,' Was dem Vorschlag Stärke und ich würde sogar sagen Brillanz verleiht, ist die verkettete Art, auf die diese Teile miteinander verbunden sind. Das Ergebnis ist ein pulsierender, vielfältiger urbaner Raum, ein kompliziertes Muster positiver und negativen Volumens, der gleichzeitig repetitiv und mehrdeutig ist. Wie eine geometrische Decke, die gleichzeitig mit drei oder vier sich widersprechenden Mustern programmiert wurde, löst die Erfindung verschiedene Lesarten aus. Sie erinnern an geläufige kontextuelle Arbeiten, an Kriers Urbanismus oder Bofills Paläste; genauer, sie erinnern an Thomas Jeffersons 'akademisches Dorf' in Charlottesville, Virginia. Farrells Absicht war es, eine neue Dorf/Stadt Typologie zu entwickeln, indem er einen einfachen Baublock in Plan und Massstab variierte. Unglücklicherweise wird dies in Vauxhall nicht verwirklicht werden, aber es ist unwahrscheinlich, dass es lange verloren bleiben wird, geht man von dem starken Interesse dieses Büros aus, Ideen ausgeführt zu sehen.

In einem Nachwort beschreibt der Autor seine zweieinhalbjährige Zusammenarbeit mit Farrell am Haus der Jencks und den Einfluss, den dies auf die Ideen beider hatte.

Eine vollständige Liste der Gebäude und Projekte und eine Auswahlbibliographie sind ebenfalls beigefügt.

Sommario

Questa monografia architettonica presenta gli edifici e i progetti di uno dei maggiori architetti britannici, Terry Farrell. La monografia è stata preparata in collaborazione con la Terry Farrell Partnership e si compone di quattro saggi, di cui due dello stesso Farrell, che illustrano la sua opera e la inseriscono nella panoramica generale.

Nel suo saggio 'L'architettura britannica dopo il modernismo', Farrell riflette sugli sviluppi dell'architettura in Gran Bretagna dagli inizi degli anni sessanta e discute sui problemi della trasformazione e dell'identità culturale nonché dello stato-e del futuro-della architettura britannica dopo il modernismo. 'Il modernismo era un movimento accentratore, la sua ideologia era quella del "stile internazionale". I contromovimenti sono regionali e le varie foci emergenti sono quelle degli architetti contemporanei come Graves, Krier, Botta, Hollein, Bofill e Isozaki. Il modernismo era impersonale, era l'architettura dell'anonimato, mentre i movimenti opposti appoggiano le idee di quegli architetti che hanno una visione e una tecnica dell'architettura altamente personale. Alla macchina estetica non ornamentale è opposta quella della decoratività e dell'ornamento; alla iniziativa maschile, la sensualità e sensitività; alle semplificazioni razionali la complessità e la contraddizione; al futurismo, lo storicismo e alla universalità delle soluzioni, è opposta la contestualità. Alla fine, il popolo britannico può anche arrivare a scoprire che uno stile più libero — 'dopo modernismo' è molto più in linea con il loro gusto dell'architettura semplicemente perché è così britannico, con il suo approccio più tollerante, più eclettico, più contestuale, più romantico, e più aperto.'

Farrell vede nella propria esperienza un allontanamento dalla filosofia accentratrice e dal fascino per la tecnologia di per sé, e un avvicinamento a un concetto che dà più importanza alla qualità della vita e in un sistema di architettura più libero e gioioso.

Nel suo saggio autobiografico, Farrell usa la nozione del porcospino e della volpe di Isaiah Berlin, per elucidare il suo progresso personale dai giorni in cui era studente a Newcastle e a Philadelphia, ad oggi; questo per quanto concerne la sua ideologia, cioè dalla filosofia del fondamentalismo appresa da Kahn fino al suo attuale eclettismo radicale. Il saggio si conclude con una illustrazione pittorica sull'argomento della figura umana come generatrice primaria della forma architettonica.

Gli edifici e i progetti illustrati mettono in rilievo in particolare il brevissimo periodo dell'indipendenza di Farrell come Terry Farrell Partnership, malgrado ci sia anche un riassunto dei lavori intrapresi in società con Nicholas Grimshaw negli anni 1965-80. I lavori includono case, edifici industriali, studi, uffici e padiglioni e mostrano una gamma di servizi concernenti non solo la conservazione e la riabilitazione degli edifici, ma anche nuove costruzioni. Ciascun edificio o progetto è ampiamente documentato con disegni, a volte sketches illustrini il concetto, e fotografie a colori e in bianco e nero

appositamente commissionate.

Colin Amery nel saggio 'Arte prammatica e virtuosità spaziale', inserisce Farrell in una classe particolare di architetti britannici la cui esperienza e conoscenza tecnica comprendono sia la tradizione inglese basata su fonti classiche, sia quella ispirata alla visione americana del mondo altamente tecnologico del dopo guerra. Amery suggerisce che a tuttoggi, la carriera di Farrell contiene in microcosmo tutto ciò che è avvenuto nell'architettura moderna. Nella esplorazione biografica che segue, Amery identifica la filosofia di Farrell di usare gli edifici come risorsa, come 'uno dei contributi maggiori che Farrell ha dato alla filosofia e al sistema dell'architettura'. I progetti più recenti (Mansion House Square e Hammersmith) mostrano un approccio delicatamente prammatico a vecchie zone della città, cioè pragmatismo inteso come reazione alla totale sottomissione agli *Zeitgeist* del movimento moderno. Grazie alla sua considerevole esperienza commerciale Farrell è stato in grado di ideare e costruire una serie di progetti che applicano la teoria delle 3 dimensioni al mondo dell'architettura del dopo modernismo.

Il linguaggio di Farrell si basa su una comprensione delle necessità ambientali (contestuali) di un luogo e nel contempo, sulla necessità di esprimere una propria idea. Prendendo l'esempio 'maestro' della gara di Vauxhall Cross, Amery cerca di definire la visione di Farrell quando all'architetto viene data la possibilità di lavorare su larga scala, e afferma che l'esempio citato mostra la crescita di un ordine razionale dalla tolleranza prammatica che fa di Farrell un architetto con un gran futuro. Altri due progetti, e precisamente Comyn Ching e la casa di Jencks, mostrano una comprensione del pittoresco e della virtuosità spaziale, nonché dell'uso del linguaggio ordinario dell'ambiente e della ricerca di un nuovo linguaggio simbolico. Un'altra qualità del lavoro di Farrell, qualità assai rara nell'architettura contemporanea, è il suo senso di giovanile divertimento.

Farrell è uno dei pochi architetti che ha incontrato favore presso il pubblico in conseguenza al fatto che egli condivide le preoccupazini della gente e protegge l'ambiente sviluppando la teoria della contestualità nei nuovi edifici. Farrell fa parte, insieme ai suoi contemporanei Jeremy Dixon e Piers Gough, di un nuovo movimento architettonico con un suo nuovo linguaggio.

Nel suo saggio 'Farrell avanza verso il simbolismo', Charles Jencks esplora le fonti del classicismo post-moderno di Farrell il quale ha superato il suo antico stile fatto di 'espedienti' o di 'ingegnose mosse intellettuali'. Avvalendozi della teoria letteraria dell'ansietà dell'influenza, Jencks dimostra che l'opinione di Farrell sulle opere degli altri architetti, costituisce un eclettismo trasformativo che si oppone al revivalismo puro. TV-am, e in particolare la chiave della volta, viene preso ad esempio della sintesi immaginativa di un classicismo di stile libero.

In un'analisi maggiormente dettagliata dei

progetti, Jencks discute delle ragioni a favore di un movimento che si allontana dalla rappresentazione per avvicinarsi all'astrazione e mostra la risultante multivalenza del lavoro di Farrell. Il progetto Vauxhall, 'la più matura affermazione dell'opera di Farrell . . . mostra una autorità competente, una trasformazione dei temi classici'. E Jencks prosegue: 'Ciò che dà forza, direi ingegno, al progetto, è il modo o ad incastro in cui queste parti sono unite tra di loro. Il risultato, è uno spazio urbano pulsante di vita, un intreccio complesso di positivi e negativi che è ripetitivo ed ambiguo al contempo. E' come un pattern geometrico programmato con tre o quattro modelli contrastanti. Una tale invenzione ispira diverse chiavi di lettura. Ricorda i lavori ambientali moderni, l'urbanismo di Krier o i palazzi di Bofill; più di tutto, ricorda il 'villaggio accademico' di Thomas Jefferson in Charlottesville, in Virginia. L'idea di Farrell era quella di inventare un nuovo tipo di villaggio/città variando un blocco di edifici basilari in piano e scala. Sfortunatamente, ciò non potrà essere realizzato a Vauxhall; ma è improbabile che il progetto rimanga a lungo nel vuoto dato il profondo interessamento di questo ufficio nel cercare di trasformare la teoria in realtà.'

Nel postscritto, l'autore annota i due anni e mezzo di collaborazione con Farrell per la costruzione della casa di Jencks e l'influsso che tale progetto ha avuto sulle loro idee.

Una lista completa di edifici e progetti e una bibliografia selezionata sono incluse.

Resumen

Esta Monografía Arquitectónica presenta los edificios y proyectos del destacado arquitecto británico Terry Farrell, preparada en colaboración con Terry Farrell Asociados, junto a cuatro ensayos, dos de ellos por el mismo Farrell, que ponen en contexto el trabajo.

En su ensayo 'Arquitectura Británica despues del Modernismo', Farrell reflecciona sobre el ejercicio de la arquitectura en Gran Bretaña desde principios de la década del sesenta y trata los problemas de cambio e identidad cultural y el estado y futuro de la arquitectura británica despues del modernismo. 'El modernismo fue centralizador, su ideología el "estilo internacional". Los movimientos de reacción son regionales y los focos dispersos que aparecen brillan con arquitectos contemporáneos que expresan su cultura, como Graves, Krier, Botta, Hollein, Bofill e Isozaki. El modernismo fue impersonal, arquitectura de anonimato; la reacción al mismo pone de manifiesto a arquitectos de visión y pericia sumamente personales. A la estética no ornamental de la máquina se responde con decoración y ornamento, a la fuerza masculina con sensualidad y sensibilidad, a la sobresimplificación racional con complejidad y contradicción, al futurismo con historicismo y al universalismo de las soluciones con contextualidad. A la larga los británicos bien podrán descubrir que un estilo más libre 'posterior al modernismo' es mucho más su tipo de arquitectura, sencillamente por ser tan británico, con su enfoque tolerante, ecléctico, contextual, más romantico y abierto'.

Farrell ve en su propia expereicia un alejamiento del credo en una filosofía centralizadora y de la fascinación por la tecnología en sí misma, hacia una preocupación por la calidad de la vida y un ejercicio más libre y placentero de la arquitectura.

En el ensayo autobiográfico del mismo nombre, Farrell utiliza la idea de Isaiah Berlin sobre el puercoespín y el zorro para ilustrar su evolución personal desde sus días de estudiante en Newcastle y Filadelfia hasta el presente; ideológicamente, desde el fundamentalismo enseñado por Kahn hasta su eclecticismo radical de hoy. Esto concluye con un ensayo ilustrado sobre el tema de la figura humana, como generador primario de forma arquitectónica.

Los edificios y proyectos presentados se concentran en el corto período de independencia de Farrell como Terry Farrell Asociados, pero se muestra también un resumen del trabajo llevado a cabo en asociación con Nicholas Grimshaw, 1965-1980. Este incluye viviendas, edificios industriales, estudios, oficinas, y pabellones, y expone una serie de trabajos que incluyen conservación y renovación, así como obras nuevas. Cada edificio o proyecto está documentado enteramente con dibujos de presentación, algunos croquis de conceptos y fotografías, especialmente encargadas en color y blanco y negro.

Colin Amery en 'Arte Pragmático y Virtuosismo Espacial' ve a Farrell como miembro de una particular clase de arquitecto británico cuya preparación incluye tanto la inglesa tradicional basada en un principio clásico como aquella inspirada por la visión americana de posguerra de un mundo altamente tecnológico. Amery sugiere que la carrera de Farrell hasta hoy pone en evidencia en un microcosmo lo sucedido a la arquitectura moderna. En el ensayo biográfico que sigue, Amery identifica la filosofía del arquitecto de utilizar al edificio como una fuente de recursos, 'una de las contribuciones más importantes de Farrell a la teoría y práctica de la arquitectura'. Los proyectos más recientes (Mansion House Square y Hammersmith) demuestran un enfoque pragmático, benigno con las viejas zonas de la ciudad; es un pragmatismo como reacción a la sumisión al *Zeitgeist* del movimiento moderno. Debido a su considerable pericia comercial, el estudio de Farrell ha podido desarrollar y construir una serie de proyectos que exponen tridimensionalmente el enfoque del estudio al mundo de la arquitectura despues del modernismo.

El lenguaje de Farrell está basado en una comprensión de las necesidades contextuales de un terreno como tambien de la necesidad de hacer aserciones formales. Utilizando el 'magistral' ejemplo del concurso de Vauxhall Cross, Amery busca definir la visión de Farrell, dada la oportunidad de trabajar en gran escala, puesto que muestra el crecimiento de un orden racional desde la tolerancia pragmática, que hace de Farrell un arquitecto con un importantísimo futuro'. Otros dos proyectos, Comyn Ching y la casa Jencks, demuestran comprensión del pintoresquismo y virtuosismo espacial, la utilización del lenguaje ordinario del contexto y la búsqueda de un nuevo lenguaje simbólico. Otra cualidad alentadora del trabajo, rara en la arquitectura contemporánea, es un sentido de diversión joven.

Farrell es uno de los pocos arquitectos populares con el público, como resultado de compartir sus intereses, protejiendo el entorno urbano y desarrollando su contextualidad en edificios nuevos. Con sus contemporáneos Jeremy Dixon y Piers Gough, Farrell es parte de un nuevo movimiento con un nuevo lenguaje arquitectónico.

Charles Jencks en su ensayo 'Farrell se acerca al Simbolismo' explora las fuentes del clasicismo postmoderno de Farrell que ha sustituído su estilo 'tech', 'útil' o 'inteligente'. Empleando el concepto literario de ansiedad de influencia, Jencks muestra que la cita de Farrell del trabajo de otros arquitectos constituye un eclecticismo transformador, en cuanto opuesto a una resposición directa. TV-am, y específicamente su clave, se da como ejemplo de una síntesis imaginativa en un clasicismo libre.

En un análisis de proyectos más detallado, Jencks expone las razones de un alejamiento de la representación hacia la abstracción y la multivalencia resultante en el trabajo de Farrell. El proyecto de Vauxhall, 'la manifestación más madura del trabajo de Farrell . . . muestra una autoridad competente, una transformación segura de temas clásicos'. Jencks continúa, 'lo que da fuerza, y diría brillo a la propuesta es el modo de trabado con que las partes se insertan entre sí. El resultado es un espacio urbano variado, latente, una configuración compleja de volúmenes positivos y negativos que es repetitiva y ambigua al mismo tiempo. Como un edredón geométrico que ha sido programado para dos o tres figuras conflictivas a la vez, la invención genera lecturas diferentes. Son reminiscencia de trabajo contextual actual, del urbanismo de Krier o los palacios de Bofill, y lo que es mas pertinente aún, evocan la 'villa académica' de Thomas Jefferson en Charlottesville, Virginia. La intención de Farrell fue desarrollar una nueva tipoligía de villa/ciudad variando un bloque básico en planta y escala. Desafortunadamente no será llevado a cabo en Vauxhall, pero es probable que no quede olvidado por mucho tiempo, adado el profundo interés del estudio en construir sus ideas'.

En una posdata el autor recuerda la colaboración de dos años en la casa Jencks y la influencia que esto tuvo sobre sus ideas.

Se incluye también una lista de edificios y proyectos y una bibliografía seleccionada.